ORPHANS

   To be an orphan by death or desertion was a hard life. Some
had good guardians and some bad. But he must have felt grand when
at 21 years of age he received his horse, saddle, bridle, a suit of
store bought clothes and one hand made, she, a bed, clothes and
furniture.

   Orphans played a great part in this Society, gave their lives
at Appomattox and Shiloh along with the rest - made inventions,
built roads, tunnels, farmed, mined and raised cattle - Wasn't it
good to be free.

GREENE COUNTY, TENNESSEE, RECORDS

Greene (now Tennessee) was formed in 1783 from Washington (now Tennessee). Washington County was formed in 1777 from the District of Washington. It was roughly the territory west of Wilkes County, North Carolina, between Wilkes and the Virginia line, which had been allowed three representatives in the General Assembly of North Carolina in 1776.

Sullivan (now Tennessee) was formed in 1779 from Washington County. Part of Washington (Tennessee) was annexed to Wilkes County, North Carolina, in 1792.

TENNESSEE

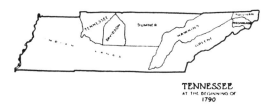

TENNESSEE
AT THE BEGINNING OF
1790

GUARDIANS & ORPHANS COURT
Greene County, Tennessee
1783 - 1883

1783 November Term
    Page 5 John Ray, Orphan of Joseph Ray decd., bound to Benjamin Ray
    to learn the Carpenter Trade until he attains to the age of 21
    years. Said Orphan now at the age of 13 years.

1784 February Term
    Page 11 Isaac Dyches, Orphan of Jacob Dyches decd., bound to John
    McCroskey to learn the Skin Dresser Trade. Said Orphan now at the
    age of 7 years.

    Page 12 William Brabson, Orphan of John Brabson decd., bound to
    Robert Fain to learn the Weaver Trade. Said Orphan now 9 years old
    next April.

1784 August Term
    Page 26 John Coats, Orphan of Joshua Coats decd., bound to Samuel
    Newell to learn the Weaver Trade until he arrives at the age of 21
    years.

    Page 26 Peter Purciful, a minor 15 years old, bound to James McAmis
    until he arrives at the age of 21 years.

1784 November Term
    Page 31 Martha Purciful bound to John Crow until she arrives at the
    age of 18 years, to learn the Weaver Trade.

1785 May Term
    Page 39 Elizabeth Phillips, a minor, bound to John Ward until she
    arrives at the age of 18 years.

1785 August Term
    Page 42 John Parkinson, Orphan of George Parkinson, bound to John
    Tadlock until he attains to the age of 21 years to learn   Trade.

1786 February Term
    Page 48 John Ray, Orphan of Joseph Ray decd., is released from his
    Apprenticeship.

1786 May Term
    Page 63 William Sutton bound to Robert Kerr Junr. until he attains
    to the age of 21 years.

1786 August Term
    Page 69 Rev. Mr. Balch is appointed guardian for 3 of his own
    children towitt, Hezekiah Washington Balch, Samuel Young Balch and
    John Franklin Balch. Anthony Moore, John Reese and David Russell
    securities.

1787 May Term
    Page 82 James Trimble, a minor now of the age of 13 next May, bound
    to John Carson until he attains to the age of 21 years to learn the
    Weaver Trade.

1788 August Term
    Page 94 David Gamble is appointed by the choice of Rhoda Chandler
    her guardian.

1788 November Term
    Page 101 Rhoda Chandler and David Gamble came before the Court
    (said Gamble being chosen guardian last Term by said Chandler) By
    consent of Court and both parties said Gamble is released.

1789 May Term
    Page 114 James Trimble, Orphan of Jane Trimble, bound to John
    Carson until he arrives to the age of 21 years. Said Orphan being
    of the age of 14 years, to learn the Linen Weaver Trade.

1

<u>1789 November Term</u>
Page 137 Dorcas Woods, minor daughter of Sarah Woods, bound to
Andrew Richie until she shall attain to the age of 18 years to
learn the Linen Weavers Trade. Said minor being now of the age of
4 years on the 15th of April next.

<u>1790 February Term</u>
Page 151 Elizabeth Berry is appointed guardian to her own children
towitt, John, Robert, Jane, Hugh, Joseph, James, Sarah and Elizabeth
Berry. Alex Outlaw, security.

<u>1790 May Term</u>
Page 157 Michael Tool, minor of Michael Tool, bound to Rudolph Boo
until he attain the age of 21 years to learn the Shoe Trade - to
give him 2 years schooling.

Page 161 Rebekah Potts, Orphan of Nathan Potts decd., bound to Jane
Calvert until she attain to the age of 18 years to learn the
Sempstor Trade. Said Orphan now of the age of 11 years.

<u>1790 August Term</u>
Page 170 Hugh Berry, Orphan of Hugh Berry decd., bound to Samuel
Jack until he attain to the age of 21 years to learn the Saddler
Trade. Said Orphan now of the age of 11 years.

Page 170 Robert and Amos Goodman, children of John Goodman,
committed to the case of John Richardson until further orders and
that Stephen and Rachel Goodman be committed to the case of Joseph
Richardson aforesaid.

Page 170 William Gallaspie and John Coteron appointed guardians to
Elizabeth and Nancy Gallaspie, Orphans of James Gallispie, decd.

<u>1791 February Term</u>
Page 193 William Smiley, Orphan of   , bound to James
Richardson to learn the Weaver Trade until he attain to the age
of 21 years.

<u>1791 May Term</u>
Page 203 John Colvin, minor, bound to Robert McCall to learn the
Weaver Trade until he attain to 21 years of age. Said Minor now
of the age of 9 years.

Page 203 Sarah Trimble, minor, bound to Rev. Robert Henderson to
learn to sew, knit and spin until she attain to the age of 18 years.
Said Minor now of the age of 7 years on the 15th July next.

<u>1791 August Term</u>
Page 208 Jeremiah Matthews is appointed (by the choice of Josiah
Leath) guardian for the said Josiah being above 14 years of age.
John Hill and George McCowen, securities.

<u>1791 November Term</u>
Page 218 George Edwards, a base mulatta minor now of the age of 7
months, bound to Archibald Roan.

<u>1792 May Term</u>
Page 240 Elizabeth Jones Mozier, bound to Moses Moore Senr. until
she arrive to the age of 18 years to learn to read distinctly and
give her a spinning wheel, a cow and calf, a chaff bed and furniture.

<u>1792 November Term</u>
Page 271 James Drain, Orphan of 10 years of age, bound to Samuel
Ellis until he attain to the age of 21 years to learn the Black-
smith Trade.

Page 271 Elizabeth Bumpas, Orphan of Job Bumpas decd., bound to
Jacob Broyles until she attains to the age of 18 years to learn
to spin, knit, sew and read. Said Orphan now of the age of 8

years in May past.

Page 271 Lettia Bumpas, a minor orphan of Job Bumpas decd., bound to said Jacob until she attain to the age of 18 years, to learn to spin, knit, sew and read. Said orphan now 4 years old.

1793 February Term
Page 273 Nancy and Martha Blackwood, orphans of John Blackwood decd., bound to John Weems. William Galbreath and John William Bowers, securities.

Page 281 James Bumpas, orphan of Job Bumpas decd., bound to John Jones to learn the Weaver Trade until he shall attain to the age of 21 years. Said orphan now of the age of 12 years last September.

1793 November Term
Page 316 James Hopkins bound to George Hopkins until he arrives at the age of 21 years to learn the Chair making Trade. Said orphan 18 years of age past last.

1794 February Term
Page 322 Joseph Hardin esqr. appointed guardian for John Hardin, an orphan child of John Hardin decd. William Davison and William Bond, securities.

Page 328 James Kenedy, a minor of Moses Kenedy, bound to James Rodgers until he attain the age of 21 years to learn the Blacksmith Trade. Said minor now of the age of 16 years and 7 months.

Page 329 John Walker bound to John Mauris until he attains the age of 21 years to learn the Wheelright Trade. Said orphan now of the age of 8 years first of September last.

1794 May Term
Page 340 Sarah Reynolds bound to John Hughes until she arrive to the age of 18 years to learn to sew, knit and spin. Said Sarah now of the age of 11 years.

1794 August Term
Page 346 Ruth Kelly, an orphan, bound to Robert Henry until she attain to the age of 18 years to learn to sew, knit and spin. Said orphan now 3 years old the third day of December next.

Page 347 James McLaughlin, a minor, bound to Philip Cole until he attain to the age of 21 years to learn the Blacksmith Trade. Said minor now 17 years first of April next.

1794 November Term
Page 360 Archibald McCaleb appointed a guardian for Jane, Mary and Elizabeth Gamble, orphans of David Gamble. James Mahan and John Hays, security.

Page 360 William Blackwood appointed guardian for Andrew Blackwood, a minor orphan. James Kersy and John Kersy, securities.

1795 February Term
Page 363 John Blair of Washington County is appointed guardian for Hugh Gamble. John Rankin and James Rodgers, securities.

1795 August Term
Page 407 David Hopkins bound to George Hopkins until he attain to the age of 21 years to learn the trade of Chair making, and to read, write and cypher as far as the rule three. Said orphan now of the age of 13 years.

1796 May Term
Page 441 Mary Goforth bound to Jesse Lynch until she attain to the age of 18 years to learn to read etc. Said orphan now of the age of 11 years past the first day of October last.

Page 442 Miles Goforth bound to Joseph Porter until he attain to
the age of 21 years. Said orphan boy now of the age of 19 the 16th
day of November last.

Page 443 Samuel Gragg and William Black appointed guardian for
John, William, Abigail and Uriah Black. James Mahan and Evans,
securities.

1796 November Term
Page 475 James Roberts appointed guardian for Samuel and Margaret
Rodgers, orphans of James Rodgers decd. James Russell esqr.,
security.

Page 476 Margaret Rodgers appointed guardian for Jane Rodgers, a
minor of James Rodgers decd. Anthony Kelley, security.

Page 477 Sarah Bumpas, orphan of Job Bumpas decd., bound to
Jeremiah Broyles until she attain to the age of 18 years to learn
to spell and read. Said orphan now being of the age of 5 years
next August.

1797 May Term
Page 33 Jemima Goforth is bound to Joseph Goforth until she attain
to the age of 18 years to learn the Sempstress Trade. Said orphan
now of the age of 5 years.

Page 33 Mary Goforth bound to Dr. William Holt until she shall
attain to the age of 18 years to learn the Miliner Art. Said
orphan now of the age of 13 years.

1797 August Term
Page 50 William Dewoody appointed guardian to Esther Dewoody, a
minor orphan. James Hayes and Benjamin McNutt, securities.

Page 63 John Newman appointed guardian for 3 boys, orphans of
William Holeman decd.

Page 69 Benjamin Bogard, orphan, bound to John Macksy Barnes until
he attain to the age of 21 years to learn the Blacksmith Trade.
Said orphan now of the age of 13 years the 10th day May last.

1798 April Term
Page 85 Ordered that William Holt be allowed 30 dollars for the
support of Hubert Weaver, an orphan, for the term of 9 months to
commence from November Term 1797.

Page 98 Abililah Barris, an orphan, bound to William Wilson until
she attain to the age of 18 years to learn to read English. Said
orphan now of the age of 4 years and six months.

Page 100 John Lester bound to Joseph Dobson until he attain to the
age of 21 years to learn the farming business. Said orphan now of
the age of 7 years the 24th day of May next.

Page 100 Mary Dobson, an orphan, bound to Joseph Dobson until she
attain to the age of 18 years to learn to spin and sew. Said
orphan now of the age of 7 years the 15th day of February last
past.

1798 July Term
Page 112 Eunice Bryan bound to Margaret Johnson until she attain
to the age of 18 years to learn to knit, sew and spin. Said orphan
now of the age of 6 years in March last.

1798 October Term
Page 130 Amee Roberts bound to Benjamin Williams until she attain
to the age of 18 years to learn to read the scriptures. Said minor
being now of the age of 7 years and 4 months and 21 days.

1799 January Term
Page 160 Reuben Lester, a natural born child, bound to Robert Dobson until he attain to the age of 21 years to learn to read, write and cypher. Said orphan now of the age of 6 years on the 25th January next.

1799 October Term
Page 192 John Roberts, an orphan, bound to Beriah Frazier until he attain to the age of 21 years to learn to read, write and cypher etc. Said orphan now of the age of 8 years in March last.

Page 192 Lettia Bumpas bound to Elizabeth Broyles until she arrive to the age of 18 years to learn to read, knit, spin and sew. Said orphan now of the age of 7 years.

1803 January Term
Page 10 Ordered that an orphan female child, daughter of Rachel Craddick decd., of the age of 4 months old now in the possession of John Jones be delivered to John Morris, esqr.

Page 14 Two orphan male children Viz William and John, sons to Rachel Craddick decd., bound to John Dodd.

Page 14 A female orphan, Drusilla, daughter to Rachel Craddick decd., bound to James Jones.

Page 14 Alexander McAlpin appointed guardian to Robert Hood. Joel Dryden and Robert McCall, securities.

1803 April Session
Page 37 William Ireland, a base born begotten child, bound to Solomon Edmundson until he attains to the age of 21 years.

Page 38 Sarah King, orphan of the age of 3 years, bound to Alexander Williams until she shall attain to the age of 18 years.

Page 54 Hannah Wright, daughter of John Wright, now in the possession of John Myers, to be delivered to Stephen Woolsey.

1803 July Session
Page 65 Margaret Purdom and William Dickson is appointed guardians of Richard Balfour, Eleanor Ewing and George Ewing Purdom, orphans of Alexander Purdom decd.

1804 January Session
Page 99 Moses Moore appointed guardian to Robert Carlisle, a minor orphan. James McPheron and James Wright, securities.

1804 April Session
Page 110 Robert Carlisle, an orphan of the age of 16 years, bound to Joel Dryden until he shall attain to the age of 21 years.

1805 January 29
Page 5 Rachel Whittenberg, a minor over 14 years of age, and James Whittenberg, a minor under 14 years of age, bound to Margaret, John and William Whittenberg, Margaret being the guardian.

1805 April 22
Page 6 Thomas Wilson appointed guardian to Lavina Simpson, a minor orphan under 14 years of age. John Wilson and Isaac Baker Senr., securities.

1805 July 22
Page 7 Samuel Koffman is appointed guardian to his daughter, Mary Koffman. Cornelius Newman, security.

1805 July 25
Page 8 Lydia Jones, a minor orphan, came into Court and chose Joseph Carter Junr. her guardian. John Jones, security.

<u>1806 January 29</u>
  Page 10 William Craddick, a minor orphan over 14 years of age,
  came into Court and chose John Dodd his guardian. Ewen Allison,
  security.

<u>1806 April 29</u>
  Page 11 George Gordon is appointed guardian to David Porter, a
  minor orphan under 14 years of age. John Shields of Cocke and
  Greene Counties, security.

  Page 12 William Conway is appointed guardian to Eliza W. Porter, a
  minor orphan under 14 years of age. Hugh Neilson, security.

<u>1806 October 28</u>
  Page 13 James M. Miller, a minor upward of 14 years of age, came
  into Court and chose Charles Lowry Senr. his guardian. James Hayes
  and William Brotherton, securities.

  Page 14 James McCollum, a minor orphan upward of 14 years of age,
  came into Court and chose Mary McCollum his guardian. Isariah
  Doty, security.

<u>1807 Page 217</u>

Henry Sevier	11 years old	14th this instant
Hundley Sevier	6 years old	4th November 1806
Elizabeth Sevier	9 years old	10th this instant
Sally Sevier	4 years old	2nd November 1806
Narcissa Sevier	2 years old	30th this instant

  Children of John Sevier are in a suffering situation and being
totally unprovided for by their sad father.
  It is ordered by the Court that the aforesaid children be bound
to Henry Conway Senr., the males until they arrive at the age of
21 years and the females until they attain to the age of 18 years.
The males to be taught to read, write and cypher to the end of the
single rule of three and the females to be taught to read, write,
knit, spin and sew. Each child to be furnished by the said Conway,
when they arrive at age, a good horse, saddle and bridle, 2 gentil
suits of wearing apparell.
  (Col. John Sevier died in 1815 - was Governor at this time. His
wife was Susanna Conway. They separated and she married Hugh
Maloney.)

<u>1807 July 29</u>
  Page 237 John Etter (age 12 years) bound to John Etter until he
  shall attain to the age of 21 years, and to be instructed in the
  art or trade of a Taylor, to read, write and cypher to the end of
  the single rule of three, and to be furnished with a good freedom
  suit of cloaths at the end of his Apprenticeship. Elizabeth Etter
  (age 11 years) and Mary Etter (age 8 years) bound to James Guthrie
  until they arrive at the age of eighteen years, to learn to spin,
  knit and sew and the duties of a good house wife, also to read
  distinctly and write an intelligible hand, and at the expiration
  of their apprenticeship to receive a feather bed and furniture and
  a good freedom suit of clothes. Rebeckah Etter (age 9 years)
  bound to John Etter until she shall attain to the age of eighteen
  years to be taught and receive the same as last above mentioned.
  And Daniel Etter (age 6 years) bound to John Rader until he shall
  attain to the age of 21 years, to learn the art or trade of a
  Waggon maker, also to read, write and cypher to the end of the
  single rule of three, and to be furnished at the expiration of his
  Apprenticeship with a good freedom suit of cloathes. The above
  mentioned children are the children of John and Mary Etter. John
  being absent upwards of two years.

<u>1807 October Term</u>
  Page 16 William Gardner, an orphan 9 years of age, bound to Jacob
  Harrison, house joiner and carpenter, until he attain the age of
  21 years. Then to be given tools and suit of clothes.

Page 29 Henry Farnsworth - $14,875 - for maintenance and clothing for Mary Miller, orphan, for 3 months.

1808 January Term
Page 44 William Caldwell, an orphan boy 16 years of age February 20, 1808, bound to Thomas Caldwell to learn Blacksmith Trade until he attain to the age of 21 years. Then to have tools and freedom suit.

Page 92 John Massa, 13 years 12th February 1806, and William Massa, 11 years 11th May 1806, bound to William Edmondson to learn carpenter and joiner trade. When finished to have set of carpenter or joiner bench tools and 2 suits of freedom cloths each.

Page 101 John Helms, orphan, bound to Thomas Murphy.

1808 October Term
Page 210 Isaac Holman, orphan about the age of 14 years, came into Court and chose Samuel Crawford his guardian. Joseph Robertson, security.

Page 219 Allen Kennedy and George W. Kennedy, orphans under 14 years, under guardianship of John Kennedy until a petition of real estate of Daniel Kennedy decd., shall be made.

Page 231 Solomon Brown, orphan aged 15 on 13th May 1808, bound to David Babb to learn the Blacksmith Trade until he attain to the age of 21 years.

Page 232 William Wright, orphan, discharged from Robert C. Gordon agreeable to Gordon and orphan's step-father, Daniel Dunnegan.

Page 237 Jonathan Ellis, orphan above the age of 14 years, came into Court and chose Laurence Earnest his guardian.

Page 243 Lewis Wheeler, orphan above the age of 14 years, chose Isaac Wheeler his guardian.

1809 January Term
Page 302 John Ellis, orphan above the age of 14 years, chose James Jones his guardian.

1809 April Term
Page 310 John Etter, orphan aged 13 years, apprenticed to John Etter - released and turned over to Robert Maloney to learn Taylor Trade.

Page 322 Edward Gladden, a mullatto male child kept by Abner Frazier, now 10 months old.

Page 323 Hannah Wright, orphan 9 years old, bound to Jesse Woolsey until she attain to the age of 18 years.

Page 323 Ibby Estep, female orphan 7 years old, bound to Henry Cross until she attain to the age of 18 years.

Page 323 Edward Gladden, orphan 10 months old, bound to John Scott until he attain the age of 21 years to learn Husbandry (if his capacity will permit).

Page 352 State vs George Starnes - beating and ill treating an orphan boy, Joseph Foshie - boy taken from his services and transferred to Simon Weston.

Page 356 John Farnsworth appointed guardian of Selena Farnsworth, an orphan under the age of 14 years.

1809 July Term

Page 387 Samuel Simons, orphan son of Betsy Simons, 18 months old 23rd of July 1809, bound to Leonard Simons until he attain to the age of 21 years.

Page 413 George McKahen, orphan 16 years old, bound to Henry Farnsworth until he attain to the age of 21 years to learn the business of Husbandry.

Page 437 Joseph Porter abuses family - Ruth Porter, age 9 on July 26, 1809, and Jenny Porter, age 5 May 1, 1809, bound to Robert McKenney.

Page 438 Peggy Garren, orphan 4 years old January 6, 1810, bound to Hugh Cavener.

Page 451 George Jewel, orphan 10 years of age, bound to Stephen Porter to learn art of a Saddler.

1810 January Term

Page 452 James W. Wyly   infant orphans under the age of
         Eliza M. Wyly   4 years of age, children of Robert
         Dorcas L. Wyly   Wyly, decd.
         Robert G. H. Wyly
         Hezekiah B. Wyly   John Russell and Valentine Sevier
         Martha H. Wyly   appointed guardians.

Page 452 Edward Gladden taken from John Scott and given to Abraham G'Fellers.

1812 July 27

Page 9 David Moore and James McAmis appointed guardians for John, Joseph, Charity, Betsy and Jonathan Milburn, minor heirs of John Milburn, decd.

1812 August 1

Page 26 James McAmis appointed guardian for the above orphans.

1812 October 30

Page 57 Sally Fernes, orphan, apprenticed to Philip Howell.

1813 January Term

Page 81 Jonathan Carder, orphan boy 15 years old, bound to Thomas Collier.

Page 84 Emanuel Dyke appointed guardian to John, Elizabeth and Anna Monger, minor orphans.

Page 91 John Carder, orphan, bound to Simon Pope.

1813 April Term

Page 130 Nancy Harmon appointed guardian to Nathan, Burton, Nancy, Bethany, Achitles and Susanna Harmon, minor heirs of George Harmon, decd.

Page 131 David Paulsel appointed guardian to Mary Brumly, minor heir of Augustine Brumly, decd.

1813 July Term

Page 157 John Maltsburger appointed guardian to George and Polly Maltsburger, minor heirs of Philip Maltsburger. Robert Hays and Michael Bright, securities.

Page 157 Franky Haynes, orphan age 1 on 27 February 1813, bound to Abraham Haynes.

1814 April Term

Page 227 Aaron Newman appointed guardian to Anthony, Nancy, Joseph, Rebecca, Honour and Cornelius Smith, miner heirs of John Smith, dcd.

Page 234 Sally Kinser, orphan age 4 on 11th January 1814, bound to
Jacob Lintz.

Page 240 Delilah Lyles, orphan, bound to Philip Evart.

1814 April 29
Page 277 Samuel Woods, orphan boy 3 years 3 months old, bound to
Aaron Williams.

1814 July 26
Page 290 Samuel Combs, orphan boy age 7 on 8 November 1813, bound
to Jacob Dyke.

1814 October Term
Page 315 Elizabeth Pope, orphan of 14 years of age, bound to
William West.

Page 326 Minor heirs of Williamson Pope, deceased, bound out

Susanna	12 years		to John Bell
Simon	7 years	22 November 1814	to Frederick Smith
Williamson	4 years	14 June 1814	to William Baley
Wiley	2 years	5 August 1814	to Mary Ann Pope
			until 6 years
John	9 years	10 September 1814	to William West

1815 January 27
Page 24 Rachel Pearcen, an orphan aged 6 years the 10th day of
April next, bound to John Robinson until she shall be 18 years of
age, to be taught to read the scriptures of the Old and New Testament, perfectly.

1815 Monday April 24th
Page 32 George Carder, an orphan boy aged 5 years on the 1st of
October last, bound to Henry French until he shall be 21 years of
age, to be taught to read the scriptures of the Old and New
Testament perfectly, to write a legible hand and to cypher as far
as the single rule of three and also the art and mistery of
Coopering.

1815 Tuesday April 25th
Page 37 Polly Lyles, aged about 11 years and 7 months, and Holly
Lyles, aged three years in August next, bound to Michael Wampler
until they shall be 18 years old, to be taught to read and write.

Nancy Lyles, aged 6 years in March last, bound to John Cobble
until she shall be 18 years of age, to be taught to read and write.

Levi Lyles, supposed to be 4 years old in October next, bound to
John Cobble until he shall be 21 years of age, to be taught to
read, write and to cypher through the single rule of three and
the art or trade of a Stone Mason.

John Ackles is allowed the sum of 30 dollars for the support of
himself and Idiot daughter one year commencing at the expiration
of the last allowance made to them.

Page 39 Solomon Willhoite is appointed guardian to Barnabas Myers,
a minor orphan. George Wells, security.

Charles Myers Senr. is appointed guardian to Elizabeth Myers, a
minor orphan. Samuel Dinsmoor and James Pearce, security.

Charles Myers Junr. is appointed guardian to Andrew Myers, a
minor orphan. Martin Lintz, James Williams and John Cook,
securities.

1815 Monday July 24th
Page 70 On motion of Michael Wampler, the Indenture by which Polly
Lyles and Holly Lyles were bound unto him by the Court, be can-

celled and that they be bound to James Ervin.

1815 Tuesday July 25th
    Page 81 William Crosby is appointed guardian to George Murrey, a
    minor orphan. Jonathan Davis and Colman Smith, securities.

    Page 82 Eleanor Murrey, a minor orphan over 14 years of age,
    appeared in Court with Robert Fristoe and chose said Robert her
    guardian. Colman Smith and Joseph Davis, securities.

1815 Thursday July 27th
    Page 102 Ordered that the Indenture by which Williamson Pope was
    bound to William Baley be cancelled and that the said Williamson
    Pope be bound to Thomas Temple.

1815 Friday July 28th
    Page 107 Polly Willoughby, aged 16 years, and Anne Willoughby, aged
    14 years, severally appeared in Court and chose James McFarland
    their guardian. James Guthrie, security.
    Also guardian to John and Elizabeth Willoughby, minors under 14
    years of age.

1815 Saturday July 29th
    Page 108 William Kelly, guardian of Jane Rodgers, an Idiot, this
    day made his annual report.

1815 Tuesday October 24
    Page 120 Preston Armstrong, a free male child of color aged 3 years
    on the 17th day of November next, bound to Robert Dobson until 21
    years of age, to be sent to school one year.

    Ordered that Elizabeth Tedwell, a female child aged 7 years and 3
    months, be bound to Andrew Hixson until 18 years of age, to be
    taught to read the scriptures of the Old and New Testament and
    write a legible hand.

1815 Wednesday October 25
    Page 126 John Gray, an orphan boy aged 17 years the 17th day of
    September last, bound to Josiah Clawson until 21 years of age, to
    have three months schooling.

1816 Tuesday January 23
    Page 152 David Frazier is allowed 18 dollars for the maintenance
    and clothing of Jefferson Faries, an orphan child.

    Page 157 Amos McBride, aged 14 years on the 20th April next, bound
    to John Delaney Junr. until 21 years of age, to be taught the art
    or trade of a Wheel Wright or making of Little Wheels, to have 6
    months schooling now and 6 months between the ages of 18 and 21.

1816 Thursday January 25
    Page 169 Alexander Steptoe bound to George Gordon until 21 years
    of age, to be taught to read the scriptures of the Old and New
    Testaments, to write a legible hand, and Arithmetic as far as
    the rule of three, and the art and mistery of Paper Making.

1816 Monday April 22
    Page 179 Anny Francis, aged 14 years and upwards, appeared in Court
    and chose James Weems her guardian. Daniel Carter, security.

    Page 185 Lorenzo D. Porter, an orphan aged 11 years in August next,
    bound to William K. Vance until he shall attain the age of 21 years,
    to be taught to read the Old and New Testaments, to write a legible
    hand and to cypher as far as the single rule of three and the art,
    trade and mistery of a Saddler.

1816 Tuesday April 23
    Page 199 Willis Hodges is allowed the sum of 75 cents per week
    for keeping a male child called Jefferson Faries.

<u>1816 Wednesday April 24</u>
Page 208 Andrew Stephens deposes that Charles Myers, Jr., Barney
Myers, Andrew Myers, Jacob Myers and Elizabeth Myers are the lawful
and only heirs of the said William Myers, deceased.

John Cook, Sr. is appointed guardian to Jacob Myers, a minor orphan
of William Myers, decd. John Cook Jr. and Martin Lintz, securities.

<u>1816 Monday July 22</u>
Page 237 Benjamin Hood, an orphan boy aged 8 years, bound to
Jonathan Newman until 21 years old, to be taught to read, write
and cypher as far as the single rule of three.

Page 238 Richard Mills, an orphan boy aged 4 years on the 9th of
April last, bound apprentice to Adam Shirley until 21 years old,
to be taught the art or trade of Coverlid Weaving, to read, write
and to cypher to the rule of three.

Reuben M. Hutchison, an orphan boy aged 15 years on the 19th day
of June last, bound to James Robinson until 21 years of age, to be
taught the farming business and to read, write and to cypher to the
single rule of three.

<u>1816 Wednesday July 24</u>
Page 257 A committee appointed to settle with James Wyly, guardian
of the minor heirs of Robert Wyly, decd.

<u>1817 January 30</u>
Page 30 Sally King bound to James McPheron Senr. - cancelled.

Amos McBride bound to John Delaney Junr. - cancelled.
Amos McBride bound to William Ross Junr. until he is 21 years old
(being now 15 years of age April next) to learn to read, write and
cypher.

By next Court, Sheriff to produce 2 children of Sally Jumps, 2
eldest children of Stacy Johnston to be provided for as the Court
thinks proper.

<u>1817 February 1</u>
Page 37 Vincent Anderson appointed guardian to Benjamin and James
Anderson, minors under age 21.

James Allen appointed guardian of minor heirs of Robert Wyly decd.
Guardianship to be settled 28 April 1817.

Sally and Comfort Ford, minor heirs of Ralph Ford decd., 14 years
of age, chose William Ford their guardian. William Hendry and Hugh
Carter, securities.

Page 51 William Blankenship appointed guardian of Edward Anderson.

<u>1818 July 31</u>
Page 132 Michael Girdner guardian of George and Nancy Girdner,
infant heirs of Michael Girdner, decd.

<u>1822 July 22</u>
Page 8 Margaret Kelley, minor orphan, bound to John Rogers. Henry
Earnest, security.

Alfred Hunter appointed guardian of Caroline Hunter, minor.

<u>1822 October 29</u>
Page 74 William and Joseph Milburn guardians to Sally, Mary Ann,
Alvina and Johnathan Milburn, minor heirs of Johnathan Milburn,
decd. Adam Fraker, security.

Wyly Johnson, orphan 6 years old, apprinticed to Watson Dudley to
learn farming.

1822 November 1
Page 83 Adam Fraker appointed guardian to Betsey Milburn. Daniel Cremer, security.

1823 January 27
Page 105 William Low, 16 years old 9 July 1822, bound to Hugh Low to learn country Blacksmith.

Page 106 John W. Farmer apprenticed to John Farmer to learn Blacksmith.

John Falls, 14 years old last August, apprenticed to Josiah Clawson to learn to be a hatter.

1823 January 29
Page 134 Peter Baker appointed guardian to Samuel, Thomas, John Wesley and Rachel Cobburn. William Smith, security.

1823 January 31
Page 141 Alexander Malone, orphan above the age of 14 years, chose William Hall his guardian. John B. Reed and Valentine Sevier, security.

1823 April 28
Page 153 William Shannon, near 17 years old, apprenticed to Richard West to learn Tanners Trade.

Sally Myers, age 5, bound as apprentice to David Moore.

Page 172 Thomas Stanfield appointed guardian to Susannah Sutton, a minor orphan. Samuel Stanfield Jr., security.

1823 May 1
Page 181 Thomas Farnsworth, 17 years old 1 August 1823, bound to Lincoln Heiskell to learn Tanners Trade.

1823 July 23
Page 192 David Kelley, male orphan - 18 years 7 February last, bound to Moses G. Wilson.

Eliza McCoy, supposed to be 5 years old November last, bound to David Kelley.

1823 July 28
Page 207 John Lands, 20 years old 18 November next, bound to George T. Gillespie.

1823 July 31
Page 219 Elizabeth Cross, 6 years old 10 January next, bound to Jane I. Craig.

1823 August 1
Page 227 Henry Montieth allowed $25.00 maintenance of John Alexander, orphan child.

1823 October 27
Page 239 John Hood, male orphan - 12 years old 1 January, apprenticed to William Hendry.

John Reeser, upward of 14 years, chose Henry Earnest, Esqr. his guardian. Thomas McMackin Jr. and John Mauris, security.

Page 240 Henry Earnest Esqr. appointed guardian to Samuel Reeser, minor orphan.

William Blair Junr. appointed guardian to Sally Wilson, minor orphan. Samuel Bowman and Frederick T. Winkle, security.

<u>1823 October 28</u>
Page 257 Jenny Ann and Sally Ripley, upward of 14 years old, chose Samuel Standfield Jr. their guardian. Joseph Johnson and Henry Ripley, security.

<u>1823 October 30</u>
Page 267 Henry Freshour appointed guardian of Dennis Dunn, minor orphan. Robert McKenney, security.

<u>1829 October 28</u>
Page 35 Alexander Pettet, orphan, bound to John Lister to learn brickmaking until he attain to the age of 21 years. To have 2 homespun suits, 1 store suit and $25.00.

<u>1830 January 25</u>
Page 73 Mary Hicks, orphan - 11 years last August, bound to Lewis Ball Esqr. until she attain to the age of 18 years.

Margaret Jane Cochran, minor under 14 - daughter of Marshall Cochran, decd., Casper Easterly appointed guardian.

<u>1830 January 26</u>
Page 89 Dennis McCoy, orphan, released from West Haworth.

Page 94 William Dunham, orphan aged 13 on 29 November 1829, bound to John Burkley to learn Saddlers Trade.

<u>1830 January 29</u>
Page 113 James Oliphant guardian to Alexander W., Nancy I., John H., William M., Eliza M. and Andrew G. Bell, minor heirs of James Bell, decd.

Page 115 Stephen Alexander guardian to Mordecai S. and Stephen T. Wyrick, heirs under 14 years of age of Jacob T. Wyrick, decd.

<u>1830 April 26</u>
Page 145 John Dinwiddie appointed guardian to his own children: Ann Eliza, James Harvey, Martha Jane, John Mauris, Sophia Stephenson, William Henderson, David Melton and Joseph Franklin Dinwiddie.

Rebecca Lard, age 9 on 10 April 1830, bound to James Matthews.

Sarah Lard, age 7 on 19 March 1830, bound to James Kirk.

Cornelius Barns, age 18 on 3 August 1831, bound to Robert Rhea to learn Blacksmith.

<u>1830 April 29</u>
Page 186 Samuel Stephens appointed guardian to William, Mary "Polly" Anne and Daniel Stephens, orphans of Andrew Stephens, Decd.

Page 187 Betsey Beals, minor, released from Jacob Beals (of Solomon). Jansey Beals appointed guardian. Jacob Beals (of Solomon), security.

John Dodd appointed guardian to William, Mary, Henry and Elizabeth Ford, minor heirs of John Ford, decd.

Polly Barnes, age 13 years, bound to Jesse Wyatt.

<u>1830 July 28</u>
Page 192 Nancy Rinehart, age 12 on September 1830, released from John Whittenberg. Bound to Isaiah Harrison.

Page 196 Rachel Dawson bound to Philip Bird.

Page 225 Rachel Black, orphan, guardian discharged.

1830 October 25

Page 250 Elias and Martha Pankey, orphans above the age of 14, chose Washington Hinshaw their guardian.

Anthony Kelley, orphan 15 years of age, chose John Robinson his guardian. James Kelley, security.

Page 251 Catharine McNew, orphan, bound to William McNew.

John McNew, orphan, bound to James McNew to learn mill-wright Trade.

Page 255 Alexander Pettit, orphan - not in Brickmaking business as intended but working for John Lister, guardian, in other business.

Page 259 Thomas McCollum 18 and Valentine McCollum 16, orphans, chose Samuel S. Hawkins their guardian.

1831 January 25

Page 331 Mary Ann McCollum, orphan - age 14, chose Samuel S. Hawkins her guardian.

Ruthy Walker, aged 3 years 1 May 1831, bound to William Whittenberg.

Polly Ann Stoffel, 4 years 14 August 1831, bound to Polly Burkey - had been bound to Andrew Stevens Jr., decd.

Page 335 Alexander Pettit, orphan boy, released from John Lister.

1831 April 28

Page 375 Samuel Stanfield guardian to Jane Ann and Sally Ripley, orphans.

1831 July 25

Page 389 Alexander Brown appointed guardian to Mary Ann Lister, orphan under 14 years of age.

Page 404 Cornelius Barnes, orphan, bound to Robert Rhea.

1831 October 24

Page 415 Robert McGee, orphan, released from Charles Bright.

Page 420 Sally Kinser - released from Jacob Lintz, guardian.

Henry, Mary and Elizabeth Ford, minors - 14 years of age, chose Mary Ford Senr. their guardian.

Page 428 Caroline Ross, minor orphan 14 years of age, chose Aiken N. Ross her guardian.

1831 October 28

Page 456 Margaret Rogers, minor above the age of 14 years, chose George Henderson her guardian.

Jonah White, minor over 14 years of age, chose Amasa Harold his guardian.

Catharine Haun guardian to her own children: Jacob, David, Christopher, Elizabeth, Catharine, Adam and Polly Ann Haun.

1832 January 26

Page 458 Albert Myers bound to John Robinson, decd. - widow Jane Robinson has him conveyed to friends in Ohio.

Page 501 Thomas Baily appointed guardian to Eveline Malinda King, minor orphan.

Isaac Walker appointed guardian to Hiram and Elizabeth Lindsay, minor orphans and heirs of John Linsey, decd.

14

1832 July 23
Page 11   Thomas Farnsworth guardian to Eliza Jane and Susan Wells, minor orphans. Peter Missemer and Jeremiah Farnsworth, security.

Page 13   Polly Hinks bound to Lewis Ball.

Humphries West appointed guardian to Robert West, infant.

Page 19   John Weems appointed guardian to Sugar Harrison, minor under 14 years of age.

1832 October 20
Page 79   William A. Hankins appointed guardian to James, Betsey and Thomas Weems, minor orphans.

1832 October 23
Page 125   Peter Whittenburg appointed guardian to James Whittenburg, orphan.

Page 127   Edward Guin, orphan, living with James Dilland.

1833 February 2
Page 183   Jacob Broyles guardian to Franklin, Wyly, Mary Jane and Elizabeth Guin, minor heirs of Daniel Guin, decd.

1833 April 23
Page 231   Thurzey Williams, minor - 10 years of age 30 March 1833, bound to John Crawford Sr.

Mary Hicks, minor orphan aged 15 in August 1833, apprenticed to Robert Wright.

Jemima Swatzel, age 14, chose James Roberts her guardian.

1833 July 23
Page 251   John McMackin guardian to Hanry, James, Sarah, Thomas, Polly and Nancy McMackin, minor orphans of Thomas McMackin, decd.

Page 262   Michael H. Basenger, 6 years 9 months, apprenticed to James D. McBride to learn farming.

1833 October 28
Page 277   Children of Michael Snider and George Hardin (5 in number) unprovided for by father:
   George Snider - 12 years - bound to John Wade, Hatter.
   Josiah R. Hardin - 7 years Sept. last - bound to Frederick M. Eller, Blacksmith.

1833 October 30
Page 286   John Gass Sr. guardian to David, William, Hezekiah B., John, George and Peggy Gass, minor heirs of John Gass Jr.

Page 298   Jonathan H. Chursant, destitute boy 16 years old in June last, bound to George King, Cooper.

Sampson Harden, destitute boy 14 years old, bound to Christopher Haun.

1833 November 1
Page 307   George Fall, aged 14 on 9 December 1834, bound to George W. Nelson to learn Blacksmith Trade.

Rebecca Large, 13 on 10 April 1834, apprenticed to William Trobaugh.

Page 308   Edmund Houp, aged 13 about 15 February 1834, bound to David Hall.

Martha Jane and Amanda Woods, orphans of William Woods, decd., bound to James Woods.

<u>1834 January 24</u>
    Page 321 Turner Smith guardian to John Alexander.

    Page 322 Andrew Smides, 2 years old in March 1834, bound to John Brannon.

    Jefferson Jackson bound to Washington Stone.

    John Jackson bound to James Marsh.

<u>1834 April 28</u>
    Page 360 Andrew I. Hail, 14 years of age, chose Enoch Hail his guardian.

    Page 371 Polly Ann Pettit, orphan, released from James Scott.

<u>1834 July 28</u>
    Page 412 Benjamin Smith, aged about 11 years, bound to James McNew to learn Mill Wright.

    Asbury and Catharine A. Bewley, upwards of 14 years, chose Catharine Bewley their guardian. Also Minerva Bewley, under 14 years, to Catharine Bewley.

    Page 414 Peter R. Rader bound to William Rader, guardian. John Etter and Vincent Jackson, security.

    Page 415 Noah Cate appointed guardian to James and Caroline Lee, minor orphans. Robert Henderson and Jesse P. Had, securities.

    Page 421 Hiram and Elisa Lindsay, upwards of 14 years, chose Farmer Pogue their guardian. Jacob Myers and John Willoughby, securities.

<u>1834 October 27</u>
    Page 552 John Johnston, minor 10 years old 1 February 1835, bound to John Anderson.

    George Spurgeon, 4 years 29 February 1835, bound to West Haworth to learn farming.

    Alexander Pettit, 12 years 21 April next, bound to Thomas Davis.

    Page 553 Mary Ann Johnston, age 6 years 10 September 1835, bound to Thomas Davis.

<u>1834 October 28</u>
    Page 469 Goulman Pratt, upwards of 14 years, chose James Tunnell his guardian.

<u>1835 October 26</u>
    Page 69 Thomas Brooks, Guardian of James Whittenberg (idiot) reports to Court.

<u>1836 January 25</u>
    Page 71 Statement of settlement made with Madison C. Snapp, Guardian of Margaret S. Murray.

<u>1838 September 3</u>
    Page 409 Statement of settlement made with James Fox, Guardian of Sarah Fox.

<u>1839 January 7</u>
    Page 6 Sarah Harris, orphan 7 years of age, bound to Alexander Kirk.

    Page 20 Daniel Trobaugh guardian to William and Anna King, minor orphans. Casper Easterly and Jacob Kerbaugh, securities.

Eliza I. Smith appointed guardian to her own children: Julie E., Clara A. and Thomas H. A. Smith. George Jones and Alexander Williams, securities.

<u>1839 March 4</u>
Page 74 Statement of settlement made with John S. McKeehan, Guardian of Patrick, Alexander, Emeline and James McKeehan.

Statement of settlement made with Robert Rankin, Guardian of Melinda Rankin and Adeline Rankin.

<u>1839 May 6</u>
Page 31 James Reese, minor 12 years old 22 August 1838, bound to Solomon Good.

Page 32 Major L. Temple and John Link guardians to Oliver P., Eleanor, William and Eliza M. Temple, minor heirs of James Temple, decd.

Page 37 George Hays guardian to John and Joshua Fincher, minor orphans. Joseph L. Hays, security.

<u>1839 June 3</u>
Page 42 Casper Easterly guardian to Thomas J., Lafayette P., Phebe E. and Margaret F. Bible, minor heirs of Thomas F. Bible, decd. John Walker, security.

<u>1839 July 1</u>
Page 56 William McDonald, orphan above the age of 14 years, chose George Montieth his guardian. Hiram Smith, security.

James Smith, orphan above the age of 14, chose Alfred Hays his guardian.

<u>1839 September 2</u>
Page 59 Madison C. Snapp guardian of Margaret S. Murray, age above 14 years, rescinded. Elizabeth S. Murray appointed guardian.

Joseph Horton appointed guardian to Wiley and Margaret Kelley, minor heirs of James Kelley, decd.

Page 84 Thomas Baily and Matilda Weems guardians to Narcissa, John G., Betsey Ann, minor heirs - under 14 years of age - of George Weems, decd. James Kenney and John Weems, securities.

Minerva, Nancy C. and George C., minors under 14 years, heirs of George Weems, decd., bound as above.

Page 86 Samuel Long, orphan 10 years old 23 January 1838, bound to David Adams.

Margaret Bridwell, 5 years on 25 December 1839, bound to Thomas Barkley.

<u>1839 December 2</u>
Page 96 Lewis I. Drake guardian to Rebecca, Eliza and Elizabeth McPherron, minor heirs - under 14 - of Andrew McPherron, decd. John Cavener, security.

<u>1840 February 3</u>
Page 110 Sarah Hankins guardian to Mary, Nancy A. and John Hankins, minor heirs of John E. Hankins, decd.

Page 112 James Ward, minor, bound to Stephen Cannon.

Page 115 Mary Jane Shanks, minor 5 weeks old this day, bound to Davis Butler.

<u>1840 April 6</u>
Page 124 Thomas Russell, colored free boy, bound to John Rankin.

<u>1840 May 4</u>
Page 137   John Jones, minor 14 years of age, bound to John
Maltsbarger.   Jacob Harden and Henry Dell, securities.

<u>1840 September 7</u>
Page 160   Abraham M. Harris, orphan 15 years old, bound to John
Ranken.

Catharine Harris, orphan 13 years old July 1839, bound to John
Ranken.

Page 162   Sarah Hawkins guardian to John E. Hawkins, 14 years of
age, rescinded.   John chose James Weems his guardian.   Jacob Myers,
security.

James Davis appointed guardian to Julia A. and Betsey Miller,
minor orphans.   Jacob Hardin, security.

Ely Gower, 5 years old 15 April 1839, bound to Ephraim Davis.

<u>1840 October 5</u>
Page 166   Elizabeth Mace guardian to William, Joseph H. and Martha
E. Mace, minor orphans under 14 years of age.

Page 167   William Cobble guardian to Margaret, Rahama, Juriah and
Louisa Mace, orphans under 14.   John Cobble and Jacob Cobble,
securities.

Page 171   Thomas Russell, free colored boy, Adam Dunwoody his
guardian.   Jesse Roberts, security.

<u>1840 November 2</u>
Page 174   William Stanfield guardian to his own children: Barton
and Catharine Stanfield, minors over 14 years old; Elizabeth Jane,
Emaline and Joseph Stanfield, minors under 14.   John Matthews,
security.

Page 177   Susan Millsteps, free girl of color, 11 months old 15
October 1839, bound to John Matthews.

Robert Reaves, 10 years old 10 March 1839, bound to John Lightner
(Blacksmith).

<u>1840 December 7</u>
Page 187   William S. and Bethia Hurley, minors above the age of 14
years, chose Thomas L. Hale Esqr. their guardian.   Casper Easterly,
security.

Indenture - Eliza I. Basinger to William Rader.
            William Basinger to John Shields.

Page 188   Robert Rankin guardian to Malinda Rankin.

<u>1841 January 4</u>
Page 196   Asbury Harrington, age 11 years 27 May 1840, bound to
Alfred H. Jones.

<u>1841 February 1</u>
Page 201   John Ross Sr. guardian of Allen, Martha, Margaret and
Mary Ann Ross, minor heirs of William Ross, decd.   John H. Ross,
security.

Elbert Merida, orphan 10 years old 14 July 1840, bound to
Johnathan R. Cook.

<u>1841 March 1</u>
Page 210   Er Babb guardian of George B., John F., William C.,
Margaret, Hezekiah B., Mary Ann and James A. Gass, minor heirs
of Hezekiah B. Gass, decd.   William Ross and Thomas Brittain,
securities.

18

1841 April 1
Page 216   George Rees, orphan 8 years old 20 December 1840, bound to David Rees.

Henry T. McCurrey guardian of Manson W. McCurrey, minor son of Joseph McCurrey, decd.

1841 July 5
Page 253   Anderson Freese guardian of Margaret Grubbs, orphan daughter of Amos Grubbs, decd.   Joseph Allen, security.

1841 September 6
Page 258   Joseph G. Gass, age 14 years 22 March 1840, bound to James W. Harrold for 4½ years.

William B. Fulks, 7 years 16 September 1840, bound to Lewis F. Self.

Page 259   Andrew J. Fulks, age 5 years last December, bound to John Dunwoody.

Page 266   Major S. Temple guardian of Oliver P., Eliza and Ellen Temple, minor heirs of James Temple, decd.

Page 267   Margaret I. Cochran, minor above the age of 14 years, chose William M. Grace her guardian.   John Sheffey and Anthony Rankin, securities.

Page 269   George Hays guardian of John and Joshua Fincher, minor orphans.

1841 September 30
Page 278   Anderson Freeze guardian of Margaret Grubs.

Page 279   David, Ann and Sally Brumley, orphans aged 14, chose David Brumley Sr., grandfather, their guardian.   Alfred and Nathan Brumley, securities.

Alfred Russell appointed guardian of Charles (over 14 years of age), Melvina, William, Laura and Elenora Brown, minor heirs of Peter Brown, decd.

Bartley Dudle, orphan boy aged 16 years 22 September last, bound to George M. Brown until he attain to the age of 21 years.

Richard Grant, orphan age about 10, bound to Cornelius Hardin.

1841 November 1
Page 285   Henderson M. Low, orphan 14 years old 19 November last, bound to David Wilson.

Ruthy Low, orphan 7 years old 6 February next, bound to James C. Wilson.

1842 January 3
Page 289   Report of a settlement made with Casper Easterly, guardian of Thomas J., Lafayette P., Phebe E. and Margaret F. Bible, minor heirs of Thomas F. Bible and his widow, Ann E. Bible, both deceased.

Page 290   Casper Easterly guardian of Margaret Jane Cochran, minor heir of Marshall Cochran.

1842 January 4
Page 302   Thomas Brooks guardian of James Whittenburg.

Page 304   Noah W. Easterly guardian of Narcissa, Sarah, Isaac and Mary Ann Easterly, minor heirs of Abraham Easterly, decd.   Jacob and Francis M. Easterly, securities.

Page 309 John Gragg, orphan 3 months old last February, bound to
James Gragg.

William Nichols, orphan 15 years old 25 February 1842, bound to
George Trobaugh.

Page 298 Casper Easterly guardian of Margaret F. Bible, minor heir
of Thomas F. Bible, decd. (6 years old)

John Dickson guardian of Charles F., William P., Malvina E., Laura
M. C. and Ellenora Brown, minor heirs of Peter Brown, decd.
William Dickson, security.

1842 March 7
Page 313 Lucinda A. Feezel appointed guardian of James H., Martin
N. B. and Lucy C. Feezel. John and William F. McBride, securities.

1842 April 4
Page 326 David Brumley - guardianship rescinded of his grand-
children: David, Ann and Sally Brumley, children of his son
William now decd.

Page 327 Jesse Wright guardian of George, Jane and Newton Rees,
minor heirs of William Rees, decd. David Rees and Jesse Ellis,
securities.

William B. Fulks, orphan, bound to John Brown.

Page 330 James Beach, orphan, bound to Lemuel Goodin.

1842 June 6
Page 336 John G. Farnsworth guardian of his own child: Mary Jane
Farnsworth, minor. Henry A. Farnsworth, security.

1842 August 1
Page 353 Noah Cate guardian of James and Caroline Lee, orphans.

1842 September 5
Page 357 James Maloy chosen guardian by Daniel G. and Eliza J.
Maloy, minor heirs, above the age of 14, of Hugh Maloy, decd.
John Love and Joseph Hutchison, securities.

George F. Gillespie appointed (by Allen) guardian of Sarah, Thomas
S. and Robert L. Gillespie, minor children of Allen Gillespie, decd.
James H. Gillespie, security.

1842 October 3
Page 363 John Harmon appointed guardian of his own children: Rufus
K. and Mordecai L. Harmon. Charles Gass, security.

1842 November 7
Page 375 Richard Grant, orphan, apprenticed to Cornelius Harden,
canceled. Bound to Thomas Murphy.

1842 December 5
Page 382 Nancy Ann Myers, minor above the age of 14, chose Isaac
Wilhoit her guardian. Samuel Wilhoit and John Love, securities.

Page 383 John Bartley renews guardian bond for Amanda McMurtry,
minor, 14 years of age. John Love and John Keyes, securities.

1843 January 2
Page 389 Martin Bridwell, orphan above the age of 16 years, bound
to David Britton.

Page 393 Two eldest children of Margaret Osburn - no person willing
to take them - Sarah Jones made apprentice to Thomas Russell (of
David) until next court.

1843 January 3

Page 397 Mecklenburg County, N.C. - Lucinda Fezell appointed guardian to her own children: James H., Martin, M. B. and Lucy C. Feezel. Lucinda's bondsmen, John McBride and William T. McBride, released.

1843 February 6

Page 401 Sarah Jane Osborne, 6 years old, bound to John D. Ailshie.

Barney McKenney, age 7 20 February 1843, bound to Henry Dyke Sr.

1843 March 6

Page 405 William Eddleman, age 10 years August last, bound to John Wright.

1843 April 3

Page 413 Jacob Jones, orphan 13 years old on 18 April 1842, apprenticed to Hiram T. Price to be taught brickmaking.

Page 423 Emeline Babb chooses her father, Samuel Babb, her guardian.

1843 June 5

Page 430 James Elbert Gosnell, orphan, 4 years old last March, bound to William Rader.

Page 431 James R. Low, orphan, 12 years old 30 May 1842, bound to Thomas Alexander.

1843 June 6

Page 437 Anderson Frieze guardian of Margaret Grubs, minor orphan of Amos Grubs, decd.

Page 441 Polly E. Saylor appointed guardian of her minor children: John and Jesse Saylor, under the age of 14 years. William Hawkins, security.

1843 August 7

Page 432 Judith Morelock chosen guardian of Anna and Henry Morelock, above the age of 14, also Matilda, Martha and Elizabeth Morelock, minor heirs of David Morelock, decd. Thomas and William Morelock and John M. Caster, securities.

James Kenney guardian of Eliza, Thomas, Henry, Amanda Jane, Malachi and George Yeakley, minor orphans of Isaiah Yeakley, decd. Robert L. Williams, security.

1843 August 8

Page 460 Mary Hail, minor orphan of Charles Hail, decd., chose John F. Wilhoit her guardian. Also guardian to Nancy Jane Hail. John R. Farnsworth, security.

1843 September 4

Page 462 James Ross appointed guardian of his 2 minor children: Margaret Jane and Ann B. Ross. Loyd Bullen, security.

George F. Gillespie guardian to Sarah S., Thomas S. and Robert L. Gillespie, minor orphans of Allen Gillespie, decd.

1843 October 2

Page 469 Christena Kesling, aged 13 on 11 June 1842, bound to George Andes.

Franklin McConnell, 12 years on February last, bound to Robert Elliott.

1843 November 6

Page 476 Susan C. Penland, 11 years old November 8 last, bound to Anderson C. Walker.

1844 Monday 1st January
    Page 5 Elam Carter, on his motion, is appointed guardian to Rachel
    Carter, a minor orphan, under 14 years of age. John Armitage and
    John McGaughey, securities.

1844 Monday 5th February
    Page 11 John Fisher appointed guardian to Rachel Carter, a minor
    orphan of William C. Carter, decd, under 14 years of age. Andrew
    McPheron, James Davis and John Armitage, securities.

1844 Tuesday 6th February
    Page 13 Polly Ann Gass, Elizabeth Gass and Joseph G. Gass, minor
    orphans and heirs of John Gass (of James) decd. and over 14 years
    of age, chose their mother, Polly Gass, their guardian. John
    Kidwell and William Gass (of John and Polly), securities.

1844 Tuesday 5th March
    Page 23 Susan C. Penland, aged 7 years on the 8th of November last
    past, bound to James Russell until she attain the age of 18 years.

1844 Monday 6th May
    Page 43 John G. Farnsworth, guardian of Mary Jane Farnsworth,
    exhibited a report of his wards estate.

1844 Monday 3rd June
    Page 47 Ezekiel Harrison, a minor orphan aged about 11 years,
    bound to Lewis J. Drake until he shall attain the age of 21 years.

1844 Monday 5th August
    Page 71 Rufus Keasling, a minor aged 10 years on the 22nd of
    February last past, bound to Elias Knipp until he attain the age
    of 21 years.

    Page 72 James E. Gosnell, a minor orphan aged 5 years, bound to
    James Evans until he shall attain the age of 21 years.

1844 Monday 6th October
    Page 91 John Gragg (of Polly) is bound to Thomas Gragg until he
    shall attain the age of 21 years.

1845 Monday 6th January
    Page 120 John G. Nelson appointed guardian of Polly Ann Farnsworth.
    John Guin, security.

1845 Tuesday 7th January
    Page 121 Reuben Keasling, a minor orphan, aged 10 years on the
    22nd day of February last past, bound to Anthony Rankin until he
    shall attain the age of 21 years.

1845 Monday 3rd February
    Page 123 Mary Jane Horn, aged 3 years on the 29th of August last
    past, bound to Mary Gass of James until she attain the age of 18
    years.

1845 Monday 7th April
    Page 144 Hiram T. Price appointed guardian of Jacob Jones, a minor
    over 14 years of age, and of Caroline Jones, a minor under 14 years
    of age. John W. Ruble, security.

1845 Monday 2nd June
    Page 155 John J. Broyles appointed guardian of Marilla Bird, Felix
    B. Bird, Melchisedec Bird and Julia Ann Bird, minor heirs of John
    Bird, decd. Jacob Seaton and Amos Bird, securities.

    Marion Wilhite appointed guardian of his two children: Mary E. and
    Oliver L. Wilhite. John W. Wilhite, security.

1845 Tuesday 3rd June
    Page 161 Green P. Miller appointed guardian of his son John N.
    Miller, a minor under 14 years of age. Abraham Naff and Thomas
    Gruner, securities.

Elizabeth Howell appointed guardian to her minor children, to wit, William, Jesse, Sarah Jane, Joseph, Elkanah, James, Thomas and Nathan Howell. John Russell, security.

1845 Monday 7th July
Page 163   Joseph M. Trobaugh appointed guardian to Charlotte A. King and William King, minors under 21 years of age. Casper Easterly and John Fisher, securities.

1845 Monday 4th August
Page 176   Robert Gray appointed guardian of Isaac B. Gray, a minor orphan. Thomas Johnson and Abner Babb, securities.

1845 Monday 1st September
Page 182   John P. Snapp appointed guardian to Martin Kennedy, Susan Kennedy, John Kennedy (over 14 years of age) and Martha Kennedy (under 14 years of age) minor heirs of Allen Kennedy, deceased. Daniel Kennedy and Levi Henshaw, securities.

1845 Monday 6th October
Page 190   On motion of George Trobaugh, he is released entirely from the Indenture heretofore executed in by order of this Court, by which a certain William Nichols was bound - it appearing that the said William Nichols, some months ago absconded and left.

1845 Monday 1st December
Page 203   Samuel S. McCurry appointed guardian of Sarah Jane McCurry. James G. Wilson, security.

Page 204   Hugh Alexander, a boy of colour, aged 12 years on the 2nd of May last, bound to Alexander Rose until he attain the age of 21 years.

1846 Monday 5th January
Page 212   David F. Hall appointed guardian of Louisa, Caroline, Samuel, Mary Ann and Thomas Brandon, minors. Jeremiah Farnsworth, security.

1846 Monday 2nd February
Page 222   Robert Donohoo, aged 17 years in July last past, bound to George Alexander, of William, until he shall attain the age of 21 years.

1846 Monday 2nd March
Page 225   Francis A. Payne, aged 17 years on the 19th of December last past, bound to Thomas Lane Jr. until he attain the age of 21 years.

William D. Dyke, aged 12 years on the 20th of March last past, bound to Allen Dyke until he attains the age of 21 years.

Page 226   Charles L. Evans appointed guardian of James A. Evans, Susan Ann Evans and Theoderick H. Evans, minor children of John L. Evans, decd. Thomas F. Evans, William Blair and James A. Evans, securities.

1846 Monday 6th April
Page 230   George W. Gass appointed guardian of Mary M., Catharine E., and Sarah J. Gass, minor orphans. John A. Stonecypher, Dutton Lane, John C. Hankins and John Kidwell, securities.

1846 Monday 1st June
Page 250   Her. D. Dyke, a minor orphan, aged 10 years in March last past, bound to Claiborn Self until he attains the age of 21 years.

Page 251   William R. Harmon, a minor orphan, aged 6 years on the 15th of November last past, bound to Isaac Black until he attains the age of 21 years.

Nancy Ann McNeese, a minor orphan, aged 4 years on the 16th of August last past, bound to Jacob Linebaugh until she attains the age of 18 years.

Polly Babb appointed guardian of Emeline, Sarah, James H., Augustus and Philip Babb, minor orphans. Charles Gass and John Armitage, securities.

1846 Monday 6th July

Page 258 Seburn Jewell and Daniel Kennedy are appointed guardians to Martha, Francis M., Alfred, Catharine, Margaret and Harriet Payne, minor children of Merryman Payne, decd. Also Mary McCleskey, heir at law of Merryman Payne, decd. John McGaughey and Reuben H. Davis, securities.

1846 Tuesday 7th July

Page 266 Mahlon Ausburn, a free boy of colour, aged 4 years on the 7th of June last past, bound to George Rector until he attains the age of 21 years.

1846 Monday 5th October

Page 280 Jacob Trobaugh appointed guardian of Maria and William Vance, minor children of James Vance, decd. William Cavener and Adam Dodd, securities.

John McMillan appointed guardian of his minor children: Isaac W., Rebecca Jane, John H. and Mary Elizabeth McMillan. John C. Dyer and Christopher Haun, securities.

George Donohoo, aged 7 years on the 10th of March last past, bound to Jacob Farner until he attains the age of 21 years.

1846 Tuesday 2nd November

Page 287 Philip, a free boy of color, aged 10 years on the 8th of March next, bound to Thomas D. Arnold Esqr. until he attains the age of 21 years, to be taught farming and to read the scriptures of the Old and New Testaments and at his freedon to receive a horse, saddle and bridle to be valued at $65.00, and two suites of good farm clothes.

William Robinson, a free boy of color, aged 1 year on the 8th of May last, bound to James Britton Sr. until he attain the age of 21 years, to be taught farming and to read the scriptures of the Old and New testaments, and at his freedom to receive a horse, saddle and bridle to be valued at $65.00 and two suites of good farm clothes.

1846 Monday 7th December

Page 294 Hugh Alexander, alias Hugh Wells (a boy of color) aged 13 years on the 2nd of May last, bound to Henry Feezel until he shall attain the age of 21 years, to be taught to read the scriptures of the Old and New Testaments.

1847 Monday 4th January

Page 304 Mary Ann Debusk, aged 5 years on the 31st of August last, bound to Elisha Debusk until she attains the age of 18 years - to be taught to read and write a legible hand - and at her freedom to have a good feather bed and furniture, a spinning wheel, a cow and calf and two suits of freedom clothes.

1847 Monday 1st February

Page 308 Eliza Coleman, a girl of color, aged 12 years on the 15th of March last, bound to Thomas D. Arnold until she attains the age of 21 years - to be taught to read the scriptures of the Old and New Testaments, and at her freedom to have one feather bed and furniture, and bedstead, one cow and calf, one spinning wheel and two suits of decent freedom clothes.

1847 Monday 1st March

Page 315 Violet Charlotty, a girl of color, aged about 5 years, bound to John Robison until she attains the age of 21 years, to be taught to read the scriptures of the Old and New Testaments, and at her discharge to receive a good feather bed and furniture, a cow and calf, spinning wheel and two suits of freedom clothes.

<u>1847 Monday 5th April</u>
Page 321   Henry Conway appointed guardian of his own children: Sarah Jane, Elizabeth and Jefferson Conway. William D. Neilson, security.

Robert R. Williams appointed guardian to Mary, Sarah and William Looney, minor children of William G. Looney, decd. William Cavener, James Britton and William West, securities.

John Freshour Jr. appointed guardian to Lydia, Nancy, Lavinia and John C. Freshour, minor children under 14 years of age. John Bowers, security.

Page 323   Farmer Pogue appointed guardian to Howel Pogue. Benjamin Williams, security.

Mahala Evans, a free girl of colour, aged 7 years in July last past, bound to Abraham Darnevon until she attains the age of 21 years.

Sarah Jane Hutton, aged 4 years on the 4th of November last past, bound to James Morrison until she attains the age of 18 years.

<u>1847 Monday 7th June</u>
Page 340   Howard K. Haworth is chosen guardian of Tilghman Ripley and Sarah Jane Ripley, minors over 14 years old - and is also appointed guardian of Lafayette, Charlotte and Josephus Ripley, minors under 14 years of age. David S. Ripley and Andrew Ripley, securities.

<u>1847 Monday 5th July</u>
Page 353   Ephraim Davis appointed guardian of Rebecca Evans and William Evans, minors. John Burkey and James Davis, securities.

Page 356   Anderson Freeze appointed guardian of Margaret Grubbs, a minor. John Matthews, Thomas Johnson and Nathan B. Johnson, sec.

<u>1847 Monday 2nd August</u>
Page 359   William A. Campbell appointed guardian of John T., Joseph M., William G. and Mary Ann Anderson, minor children of William Anderson, decd. John Maloney and Josiah McMillan, securities.

<u>1847 Monday 6th September</u>
Page 361   John J. Broyles appointed guardian of Mary Ann, Madison, Barbary, William J., Henry H. Barnhart, Rachel Cannon, Rebecca Cannon and Marilla Alexander, minor orphans. William Cannon and Felix Barnhart, securities.

Thomas Self Jr. appointed guardian of James G. W. Courtney, a minor. William A. Campbell, security.

William A. Campbell appointed guardian of Thomas, Daniel and Ruth Ann Wood, minor orphans. Thomas Self Jr., security.

<u>1847 Monday 4th October</u>
Page 372   Richard Petit, aged 7 years on the 4th of April last past, bound to John Haun until he attains the age of 21 years.

<u>1847 Tuesday 5th October</u>
Page 373   Elizabeth Stonecifer and Henry Stonecifer, minors over 14 years of age, chose Henry Marsh Sr. their guardian. Gravner Lickens, security.

<u>1847 Monday 1st November</u>
Page 376   Jacob Newman, a minor over 14 years of age, chose Joseph Bowman as his guardian. Dutton Lane, security.

Page 377   John W. K. Doak appointed guardian of Elizabeth Looney, a minor. William West, security.

<u>1847 Monday 6th December</u>
Page 381   Minerva Pinkston, aged about 7 years, bound to Francis Pinkston until she attains the age of 18 years.

Julia Ann Burrus, a free coloured child, aged 2 years on the 22nd of December last past, bound to Jeremiah Halaway until she attains the age of 21 years.

Page 383   Thomas Self Sr. appointed guardian of Sarah Jane Burkey, a minor.   Claiborn Self and Thomas Self Jr., securities.

Page 384   Sarah Jane Mecler, aged about 8 years, bound to John Morris until she attain the age of 18 years.

1848 Monday 3rd January

Page 387   John Cobble appointed guardian of Catharine D., Caroline, Martha M. and John A. Bowers, minor heirs of Jonas Bowers, decd. Jackson Mace and John Harmon, securities.

Page 392   John Pinkston, aged about 8 years, bound to William W. Drake until he attains the age of 21 years.

1848 Monday 7th February

Page 399   Bluford Russell, aged about 10 years, bound to John Laney until he attains the age of 21 years.

Page 402   Thomas A. Beach, aged 7 years on the last day of May last past, bound to Mary Dodd until he attains the age of 21 years.

Page 403   Alexander Parken, aged 15 years on the 20th of June last past, bound to Allen English until he attain the age of 21 years.

Cornelius Hardin appointed guardian of Patsy O. Hardin, a minor orphan.   Eliakim Cox and John Davis, securities.

1848 Tuesday 7th March

Page 407   Joseph Wolf, aged 5 years on the 7th of August last past, bound to Benjamin Dyche until he attains the age of 21 years.

Page 408   Elihu Linebaugh appointed guardian of Nancy Ann McNeese. James D. Dickson, security.

1848 Monday 5th June

Page 458   George Kenney appointed guardian of Peter, Maria, Mary Ann and Jacob Couch.   Ephraim Carter, Calvin Smith and John A. Couch, securities.

William Jones appointed guardian of John A. Ross, a minor heir (under 15 years of age) of John Ross, decd.   John Davis, security.

Alexander McPheron appointed guardian of Rachel Carter.   Absalom D. Haworth, security.

1848 Monday 3rd July

Page 466   William Boyce appointed guardian of William C. and Warren S. Hunt.   Frederick Smith and John Maloney, securities.

1848 Tuesday 4th July

Page 479   Thomas Buster, a free colored boy, bound to James Britton until he attain the age of 21 years.

Sarah Ann Hutton, a free colored girl, bound to Mary Dodd until she attain the age of 21 years.

1848 Monday 7th August

Page 482   Sarah J. Mecler, aged about 8½ years, bound to David Bird until she attain the age of 18 years.

James A. Evans appointed guardian of Hester Isabella Boyd.   John Shields, security.

1848 Monday 4th September

Page 486   William Ross of Allen appointed guardian of Nancy Ross, James Ross and Margaret Ross, minor heirs of Allen Ross, decd. Cornelius Hardin and James Weems, securities.

Elephalet Barlow appointed guardian of Andrew J. and William Brotherton, minors.   George Kenney and Claudius B. Walker, securities.

Page 487   Mahala Harris, aged about 14 years, bound to John Kidwell until she attain the age of 18 years.

William Looney, aged 10 years in February last past, bound to James W. Harrold until he attains the age of 21 years.

Rose Harris, aged about 9 years, bound to William B. Hutson until she attains the age of 21 years.

William E. Harris, aged about 7 years, bound to John McBride until he attains the age of 21 years.

1848 Monday 2nd October
Page 490 Frederick Smith appointed guardian of Anna Smith. George Smith of Frederick and John McAmis, security.

1848 Monday 6th November
Page 500 Robert M. Barton and Charles P. Nenney appointed guardians of William W. Barton. Robert J. McKenney, security.

Page 502 Nancy Kesterson appointed guardian of Thomas and Patrick H. Kesterson. Charles Kesterson, Uriah Kesterson, William C. Kesterson and Dan J. Kesterson, securities.

William Winkle, aged 8 years on the 9th of April last past, bound to John A. Carter until he attains the age of 21 years.

Joseph Reynolds, aged 8 years on the 23rd of January last past, bound to Archibald McAfee until he attains the age of 21 years.

1849 Monday 1st January
Page 4 William Thomas, aged 18 years on the 5th day of August last past, bound to John Matthews esqr. until he attains the age of 21 years.

Page 5 William M. Grace appointed guardian of John M., Amanda and William G. Dunlap, minors over 14 years of age. James C. Wilson, security.

1849 Tuesday 2nd January
Page 6 Bluford Russell, aged about 11 years, bound to Samuel Ottinger until he attains the age of 21 years.

1849 Monday 5th February
Page 7 James M. Spurgen, a minor, aged 16 years on the 9th day of January last past, bound to James Smith until he attains the age of 21 years.

Page 10 Anderson W. Walker appointed guardian of Elizabeth, Robert, Henry V., Sally R. and Emily McKenny, minors. Henry B. Baker and Nancy McKenny, securities.

1849 Tuesday 8th May
Page 25 Richard Noah, aged 6 years on the 15th of this month, bound to Washington Lauderdale until he attains the age of 21 years.

Polly Ann Dyche, aged 3 years in August last past, bound to James H. Foster until she attains the age of 18 years.

1849 Monday 4th June
Page 26 John Russell appointed guardian of William, John, Rebecca, __?__, Bluford and Susan Russell, orphan children and heirs at law of James Russell, decd. William F. McBride and William P. Sharp, securities.

1849 Monday 2nd July
Page 29 Uriah T. Walden, aged 8 years on the 26th of August last past, bound to Joseph Black until he attains the age of 21 years.

Andrew J. Jeffries, aged 13 years in September last past, bound to Joseph Rodgers until he attains the age of 21 years.

Page 30 Seth Babb appoinged guardian of Annise O. Pickering, Susannah Hunt and Samuel G. W. Gaunt, minors over 14 years of age, also John F. Gaunt and Ely Alvenzey Gaunt, minors under 14 years of age. James M. McCollum and Abner Frazier, securities.

1849 Monday 6th August
    Page 37   Jacob Justis appointed guardian of Hannah Smith, minor.
    Loyd Bullen and James Williams, securities.

1849 Monday 5th November
    Page 49   Andrew Walden, ali s Gillet, bound to Jackson Campbell
    until he attains the age of 21 years.

    Margaret Walden, alias Gillet, aged about 7 years, bound to Henry
    T. McMillan until she attains the age of 18 years.

1849 Monday 3rd December
    Page 54   Rebecca Lane appointed guardian of William T. Lane, John P.
    Lane and Sarah Jane Lane, minors.   John Haun Sr. and Seymour Haun,
    securities.

1850 Monday 7th January
    Page 57   William R. Neilson appointed guardian of Catharine A.
    Neilson.   Charles S. Neilson, security.

    William C. Maloney appointed guardian of Abraham B. Easterly, a
    minor.   Reuben Easterly, security.

1850 Monday 4th March
    Page 64   John Crum appointed guardian of his wife Elizabeth Crum, a
    minor.   Samuel W. Davis, security.

    John R. Moore appointed guardian of John L. and Susan E. Moore,
    minor heirs of Jeremiah Moore, decd.   David M. Dobson and Edmund
    B. Miller, securities.

1850 Monday 1st April
    Page 81   Miranda, a free girl of color, aged 4 years in February
    last, bound to John A. Stonesifer until she attains the age of
    21 years.

1850 Monday 6th May
    Page 87   John Gregg (long) appointed guardian of Lucy Ann Morrison,
    a minor.   Samuel H. Shrewsberry, security.

    Alexander Osburn, aged 10 years in January last past, bound to
    Daniel Britton until he attains the age of 21 years.

1850 Monday 3rd June
    Page 90   John Wolf, aged about 6 years, bound to Joseph Cobble until
    he attains the age of 21 years.

1850 Monday 5th August
    Page 100   Elihu B. Simpson appointed guardian of Felix F., Mary
    Jane, Elias, Jonathan R., Elizabeth, Joseph and Robert Simpson,
    minor heirs of Elias B. Simpson.   Elias B. Simpson and James
    Simpson, securities.

1850 Monday 2nd September
    Page 104   William S. McGaughey and Richard W. McGaughy appointed
    guardians of Catharine, Margaret E., Nancy J., Mary Ann and Martha
    McGaughy, minor heirs of David and Jane McGaughy.   Thomas Alexander
    Jr. and Samuel McGaughy, securities.

1850 Monday 9th October
    Page 107   Thomas Dodd appointed guardian of his minor children:
    William C., John P., Jacob E., Mary A., Thomas McK. and Richard
    W. Dodd.   Thomas Bailey and John McBride, securities.

    John Kimmons appointed guardian of Elizabeth, John, Caroline and
    Amanda Engledow, minor heirs of Hiram Engledow, decd.   Richard
    Engledow, security.

    Page 112   Elvira Merida, a minor orphan over 14 years of age, chose
    John W. Sisk as her guardian.

1850 Monday 4th November
Page 114 Abijah Scruggs appointed guardian of John Brown. W. C.
Maloney and Christian Bible, securities.

1850 Monday 2nd December
Page 118 Willet Mohog, aged 3 years on the 24th of December last
past, bound to Jonathan R. Cook until he attains the age of 21
years.

Mary A. Ross, a minor over 14 years of age, chose Alfred Armitage
as her guardian. Vincent Anderson, security.

1851 Monday 6th January
Page 121 Alexander Hall appointed guardian of his minor children:
Susan, William and Margaret Hall. Joseph H. Smith and Robert
Henderson, securities.

Page 122 Anna S. Smith appointed guardian of her minor children:
Lavina and William Smith. Allen Baker and Coalman Smith, securities.

William Bible appointed guardian of Clarissa Bible. Josiah C.
Debusk and Blackstone McDannel, securities.

1851 Monday 3rd March
Page 132 John Rankin appointed guardian of William C. and Warrenton
S. Hunt, minor heirs of Adam P. Hunt, decd. David R. Johnson and
Robert Rankin, securities.

1851 Tuesday 4th March
Page 136 Matthew Goodin, aged 12 years on the 13th day of February
last past, bound to James Evans until he attains the age of 21 years.

William Looney, aged 13 years on the 9th day of February last past,
bound to John Crum until he attains the age of 21 years. Samuel W.
Davis, security.

Hiram Price, aged 12 years on the 8th day of March last past, bound
to James Woolsey until he attains the age of 21 years.

1851 Monday 5th May
Page 147 Cornelius Smelser appointed guardian of Lydia R. Smelser.
John Renner Jr. and Charles L. Evans, securities.

1851 Monday 7th July
Page 155 Minerva Scruggs appointed guardian of John A., Reese P.
and Albert B. Scruggs, minor orphans. Samuel H. Shrewsberry and
Henry A. Farnsworth, securities.

John McAmis appointed guardian of Hannah Ann and John Stanfield,
minors. Jesse Wright, security.

John Burkey appointed guardian of his daughter Sarah J. Burkey.
Ephraim Davis, security.

1851 Monday 1st September
Page 171 Mary Emily Gosnell, alias Taylor, aged 3 years on the 17th
of November last past, bound to John W. Taylor until she attains
the age of 18 years.

Page 174 Abraham Stonesifer appointed guardian of his two minor
children: Sarah E. and Martha J. Stonesifer. Loyd Bullen, Charles
Hays and John A. Stonesifer, securities.

Joseph Wolf, aged 9 years on the 7th day of August last past, bound
to Jacob Easterly until he attains the age of 21 years.

William Marvel and Abraham Hays, minors over 14 years of age, chose
Britton Hayes as their guardian. Isaac A. Allen, security.

1851 Monday 6th October
Page 184 Bayles Jones appointed guardian of Elizabeth Looney.
David R. Johnson and Samuel Oliphant, securities.

William Evans, aged 7 years, bound to James G. Reaves until he
attains the age of 21 years.

Page 190 William West appointed guardian of Mary, Sarah and William Looney, minor heirs of William G. Looney, decd. Seburn Jewel, sec.

1851 Monday 3rd November
Page 193 Talitha C. Scott, aged 9 years on the 31st of August last past, bound to Thomas J. Slater until she attains the age of 18 years.

1851 Monday 1st December
Page 210 Felix W., Kitty E., Narcissa V. and Joseph S. F. Earnest, minor orphans over the age of 14 years, chose Isaac N. Earnest as their guardian. Isaac N. Earnest also appointed guardian of Jacob P. Earnest, a minor under 14 years of age. Isaac Earnest and Joseph W. Earnest, securities.

1852 Wednesday 7th January
Page 229 Alexander R. Alexander appointed guardian of Mordecai L. Barton, a minor and legatee of M. Lincoln, decd. William Barton and David G. Vance, securities.

1852 Monday 2nd February
Page 230 James Russell, a colored boy, aged about 12 years and 6 months, bound to William Johnson until he attains the age of 21 years.

1852 Monday 1st March
Page 238 George W. Harmon, aged 9 years in October last past, bound to Jeremiah Prather until he attains the age of 21 years.

Thomas Russell, a colored boy, aged 13 years on the 10th of May last past, bound to Joseph Johnson until he attains the age of 21 years.

Page 244 William Looney, a minor heir of William G. Looney, decd., and being above the age of 14 years, chose John Crum as his guardian. Samuel W. Davis, security.

1852 Monday 5th April
Page 264 John H. Hays appointed guardian of Harvey, Franklin and Amanda Jane Philips, minor children of Royal Philips, decd. John Tadlock and Thomas Hays, securities.

1852 Tuesday 6th April
Page 269 James Britton Jr. appointed guardian of Francis Boggs. S. P. Crawford and Joseph B. Dobson, securities.

William R. Bryan appointed guardian of Ruth Ann, Thomas F., Daniel M. and Sarah E. Wood. William C. Maloney, George Jackson and James Kirk, securities.

1852 Monday 7th June
Page 279 William Francis Lauderdale, aged 2 years on the __ of January last past, bound to James Lauderdale, until he attains the age of 21 years.

Catharine Brown, a mullatto girl, aged 4 years on the 30th of June last past, bound to Samuel B. McCookle until she attains the age of 21 years.

1852 Monday 2nd August
Page 293 James Hutcheson appointed guardian of Eliza Jane Hutcheson formerly Eliza'Jane Henegar, alias Grieron?, minor heir and legatee of William Henegar, decd. Joseph Hutcheson, security.

John Wolf, aged 8 years on the 15th of June last past, bound to John Hall until he attains the age of 21 years.

1852 Monday 6th September
Page 302 George Emmett, aged 8 years on the 10th of June last past, bound to Claiborn Self until he attains the age of 21 years.

Viney Lane, a colored girl, aged 11 years, bound to Washington Stone until she attains the age of 21 years.

Page 308   Samuel H. Baxter appointed guardian of Andrew J. and Mary E. Beals, minors. Hail Baxter, security.

John F. Gass appointed guardian of Hesekiah B., Mary Ann and James Gass, minors. Loyd Bullen, John Kidwell and George M. Gass, sec.

Reuben West Jr. appointed guardian of Rhoda English, a minor. James Shanks, security.

1852 Monday 4th October
Page 310   Shadrick S. Babb appointed guardian of Philip Hutson Babb, a minor heir of Philip Babb, decd. George Kinney and James Williams, securities.

1852 Monday 4th October
Page 320   Samuel S. M. Doak appointed guardian of _____ Johnson and _____ Johnson, minor children of James Johnson, decd. John W. K. Doak, security.

1852 Tuesday 2nd November
Page 332   John Simpson, aged 5 years in April last past, bound to George M. Spencer until he attains the age of 21 years.

1852 Monday 6th December
Page 335   James Britteen appointed guardian of David Wallace, Eliza Russell, William Russell, Adaline Russell, Sarah Russell and David Russell, minors. Thomas Russell, security.

1853 Monday 7th February
Page 360   Henry A. Farnsworth appointed guardian of Thomas Franklin Johnson and Mary Elizabeth Johnson, minor heirs of James Johnson, decd., S. S. M. Doak the former guardian having resigned his guardianship. M. S. Temple and Isaac F. Lamons, securities.

Solomon Dudley, a minor over 14 years of age, chose Bartley F. Dudley as his guardian. Francis Dudley, security.

Page 361   Anderson W. Walker appointed guardian of William Dunlap, a minor over 14 years of age, who has chosen him. George W. C. Dunlap and Henry B. Baker, securities.

1853 Monday 7th March
Page 369   Henry B. Harrison appointed guardian of Sarah Ann Harrison, a minor. Daniel Britton, security.

Wilson McAmis appointed guardian of Jacob H. Brener, a minor. Nathan Dodd, security.

John Henry Houts, aged 3 years in May last past, bound to Aaron Archor until he attains the age of 21 years.

Margaret Elizabeth Lyon formerly Margaret E. McGaughy, a minor over the age of 14 years, chose Chittenden M. Lyon as her guardian. James B. Lyon and Sam Milligan, securities.

Joshua Jones, aged 16 years, bound to Edmund B. Miller until he attains the age of 21 years, with the understanding that if said boy who is a cripple becomes unable to work at his trade, the Indenture is to be recinded.

1853 Monday 4th April
Page 383   James Sizemore, aged 7 years, bound to James W. Galbreath until he attains the age of 21 years.

1853 Monday 2nd May
Page 392   Cain Broyles appointed guardian of Roswell E., Eugene T. and Emilins F. Kingsley, minors. George W. Houte, security.

Abraham B. Dyer appointed guardian of Sarah Dyer, a minor. John C. and John S. Dyer, securities.

1853 Monday 6th June

Page 394 Watson W. Varner, a minor over the age of 14 years, chose Montgomery Stuart as his guardian. Samuel H. Shrewsberry, security.

Catharine Kennedy (formerly) Catharine McGaughey, a minor, chose James Kennedy as her guardian. Samuel McGaughey and William S. Kennedy, securities.

1853 Tuesday 7th June

Page 399 Mary Emily Gosnell, aged 4 years on the 18th of November last past, bound to Jesse Gosnell until she attains the age of 21 years.

1853 Monday 4th July

Page 400 Samuel Morelock Sr. appointed guardian of William, Robert and David Craddick, minors. Samuel Morelock Jr., security.

1853 Tuesday 5th July

Page 411 Charles Miller, aged 9 years in July 1853, bound to Robert Mason until he attains the age of 21 years.

1853 Monday 1st August

Page 413 Lydia Gahagan appointed guardian of Julia J. and William W. Gahagan, minors under 14 years of age. George W. Foute, sec.

James H. Bright appointed guardian of Martha Ruttedgo? Carson, a minor heir of William A. Carson, decd. Loyd Bullen, security.

Eli Warrick, a colored boy aged 3 years on the 10th of August 1853, bound to Jane Kennedy, a free woman of color, until he attains the age of 21 years.

1853 Monday 5th September

Page 419 Seymour Pettitt, aged 6 years in August last past, bound to Uriah Kesterson until he attains the age of 21 years.

Elizabeth Brown, aged 12 years on the 1st day of the present month, bound to William Boyce until she attains the age of 19 years.

Page 421 Robert Catron appointed guardian of Barbara Ann and Martha Jane Catron, minors. John Catrons and Henry Toby, securities.

William Shields appointed guardian of Thomas F. Evans, a minor. John Shields, James Biggs and James Shaw, securities.

Daniel Allen appointed guardian of William, James, Samuel and Caroline Allen, minors. James Allen, security.

1853 Monday 3rd October

Page 435 James Dunahoo, aged 9 years on the 31st of October 1852, bound to John Maloney until he attains the age of 21 years.

1853 Monday 7th November

Page 437 Benjamin Golden appointed guardian of Samuel P,, Elijah, Benjamin N., Cathrine and George E. Golden, minors. Samuel Henry, security.

Anderson W. Walker appointed guardian of Hiram J., Martha M., Mary E., Nathan W. and Harriet Levania Cogburn, minor heirs of John Cogburn, decd. Samuel Henry, security.

George Donohoo, aged 14 years on the 10th of March last past, bound to James M. Lowry until he attains the age of 21 years.

Susan Donohoo, aged 6 years in November instant, bound to Samuel R. Oliphant until he attains the age of 21 years.

1853 Monday 5th December

Page 447 Martha Leticia Brown, aged 10 years on the 31st of May last past, bound to Mary Ann Rose until she attains the age of 21 years.

William Morgan Miller, aged 10 years in June last past, bound unto William D. McLellan until he attains the age of 21 years.

Page 448　George Anderson Chamless, a minor over 14 years of age, chose Henry McCoy as his guardian.

William Rader and Mary Rader, minor heirs of John Rader, decd., over 14 years of age, chose Samuel Rader as their guardian. James M. Rader, security.

1853 Tuesday 6th December
Page 451　George Donahoo, aged 14 years in March last past, bound to James M. Lowry until he attains the age of 21 years.

1854 Tuesday 3rd January
Page 460　William Evans, aged 10 years, bound to James Wright until he attains the age of 21 years.

1854　Monday 6th February
Page 464　William C. Neil appointed guardian of Caroline Neil, a minor heir of Stoddart Neil, decd. William S. White, security.

Page 465　Nancy Jane Neilson, a minor over 14 years of age, heir of William Neilson, decd., chose E. B. Miller as her guardian. James C. Wilson, security.

1854 Monday 6th March
Page 471　Adam P. Campbell appointed guardian of Margaret Campbell, formerly Margaret Grubbs, a minor. Jacob Austise, security.

Page 472　Elvira Rankin and Robert Rankin appointed guardians of Mary E., Nancy J., Alexander B. and Charles A. Rankin, minor heirs of Thomas C. Rankin, decd. Seburn Jewel, security.

1854 Monday 3rd April
Page 22　James Dunwoody appointed guardian of Eliza, William, Sarah, Susan and David Russell, minor heirs of James H. Russell, decd. William Dunwoody and Thomas Russell, securities.

Augustus F. Broyles appointed guardian of Julia Ann Broyles, formerly Julia Ann Bird, a minor. Mason K. Jones and G. J. Broyles, sec.

1854 Tuesday 4th April
Page 26　Edmund Jackson, a free boy of colour, aged 17 years in January last past, bound to Abraham Damron until he attains the age of 21 years.

Thomas Lane Sr. appointed guardian of Mary, Martha and James Lane, minors. Joshua C. Lane, security.

1854 Monday 1st May
Page 31　Alexander Williams, aged 6 years on the 11th of April last past, bound to Joseph Brunner until he attains the age of 21 years.

1854 Monday 5th June
Page 36　James M. Marshall, a minor heir of Joseph Marshall, decd., over the age of 14 years, chose James Tame as his guardian. Thomas Tame, security.

Page 37　Elizabeth Carter, a minor over the age of 14 years, chose John T. Carter as her guardian. Dazzle Carter, security.

1854 Monday 3rd July
Page 42　Nancy Carter, formerly Nancy Wattenbarger, a minor over the age of 14 years, chose Jacob Justis as her guardian. George Kenney, security.

Page 43　John Crawford appointed guardian of Polly, Samuel, James D., A. Julian, Martha, Virginia and Thomas Frazier, minor heirs of Abner Frazier, decd. John Rankin, security.

1854 Monday 7th August
Page 53　David S. Ripley appointed guardian of Joseph Ripley, a minor heir of Samuel Ripley, decd. Howard K. Haworth, security.

John Crabtree appointed guardian of Thomas Russell Creamer and Virginia Adaline Creamer, minor heirs of Thomas Creamer, decd. Martha Creamer (their mother), security.

1854 Monday 4th September
Page 59 Samuel P. Myers appointed guardian of Sarah, Elizabeth and Alfred Carter, minors. Elam Carter, security.

Page 60 Martha Leticia Brown, a free girl of color, aged 11 years on the 31st of May last past, bound to Robert Mason until she attains the age of 21 years.

1854 Monday 2nd October
Page 65 John Willoughby appointed guardian of Elijah Willoughby and John McFarland, minors. Jacob Myers and Farmer Williams, securities.

Page 66 Jacob Farmer appointed guardian of John P., David N. and William J. Cloyd, minors. James Davis, security.

1854 Monday 6th November
Page 78 Benjamin F. Yoe appointed guardian of James Layfayette Pinkston and Adison Pinkston, minors. John Wright and William M. Williams, securities.

Jacob Litrell appointed guardian of Mary Elizabeth Litrell, a minor. John Shields and Alfred Brumley, securities.

Page 79 William Nichols, a free boy of color, aged 19 years, bound to Samuel B. McCorkle until he attains the age of 21 years. B. McDannel, security.

1854 Tuesday 7th November
Page 88 Alexander Osburn, aged 14 years in January last past, bound to Joseph R. Dunwoody until he attains the age of 21 years. John Gass, security.

1854 Monday 4th December
Page 92 Jesse S. Reeve appointed guardian of Joseph S. T. and Narcissa Virginia Earnest, minors. Jesse R. Earnest, security.

1854 Tuesday 5th December
Page 95 Edward H. West appointed guardian of David R. West, a minor. William West, security.

1855 Monday 1st January
Page 98 John J. Broyles appointed guardian of Keziah Elizabeth Broyles, minor heir of Ephraim B. Broyles, decd. Nelson S. Broyles and James Jones, securities.

1855 Tuesday 2nd January
Page 108 Mahlon Osburn, a boy of color, aged 12 years on the 17th of July last past, bound to John S. Love until he attains the age of 21 years. George Rector, security.

1855 Monday 5th February
Page 113 John J. Broyles appointed guardian of Felix E. and Mary Painter, minor heirs of William Painter, decd. Thomas Painter and Nelson S. Broyles, securities.

Page 114 Michael Dearstone appointed guardian of Lorenzo, William and Marcus Porter, minor heirs of John Porter decd. A. W. Walker, security.

James McCollum appointed guardian of Thomas F., Elizabeth Elvira and Jacob Williams, minor heirs of J. Allen Williams, decd. Wyly Campbell, security.

Levina Love, a free girl of color, aged 6 years in December last past, bound to Charles F. Brown until she attains the age of 21 years. David Sevier, security.

Anderson Love, a free boy of color, aged 6 years on the __ day of this instant, bound to Charles F. Brown until he attains the age 21 years. Davis Sevier, security.

<u>1855 Tuesday 6th February</u>
Page 120 Sally Coleman, a free girl of color, aged 1 year on the
19th of March last past, bound to Thomas D. Arnold until she attains
the age of 21 years. William Hawkins, security.

<u>1855 Monday 5th March</u>
Page 129 Josiah Hinkle, aged 14 years in June last past, bound to
Peter Huff until he attains the age of 21 years. Andrew J. Rhea,
security.

John Hinkle, aged 13 years on the 7th of July last past, bound to
Jacob H. Feazell until he attains the age of 21 years. Peter Huff,
security.

Elijah Hinkle, aged 8 years on the 14th of June last past, bound to
Jonathan Debush until he attains the age of 21 years. J. C. Debusk,
security.

Harriet Hinkle, aged 6 years on the 18th of August last past, bound
to Margaret Ren until she attains the age of 18 years. Jacob H.
Feazell and Peter Huff, security.

<u>1855 Monday 2nd April</u>
Page 139 Conzada, a free girl of colour, aged 16 years, bound to
James Britton Sr. until she attains the age of 21 years. Sam
Milligan, security.

George Washington Simpson, aged 6 years on the 7th of August last
past, bound to Jeremiah McMillan until he attains the age of 21
years. C. C. McMillan, security.

Jane Harris, a free girl of color, aged 12 years, bound to John
Maloney until she attains the age of 21 years. V. S. Maloney,
security.

Mariah Lowry, aged 11 years on the 10th of April 1855, bound to
John W. K. Doak until she attains the age of 18 years. Lewis
Rankin and James W. Galbreath, security.

<u>1855 Tuesday 3rd April</u>
Page 154 Elizabeth Hinkle, aged 9 years on the 7th of September
last past, bound to Anthony Rankin until she attains the age of
18 years. Peter Huff and J. H. Feazell, securities.

It appearing to the satisfaction of the Court that there was an
error in the ages of John Hinkle, who was bound to Jacob H. Feezell,
also of Elijah Hinkle, who was bound to Jonathan Debusk, and also
Josiah, who was bound to Peter Huff. The proper and true ages of
said children vis. Elijah Hinkle, aged 7 years on the 8th of June
last past, and Josiah Hinkle, aged 13 on the 6th of February last
past, and John Hinkle, aged 11 years on the 7th of June last past.

<u>1855 Monday 7th May</u>
Page 157 George Dunahooe, aged 16 years in March last past, bound
to William D. McLelland until he attains the age of 21 years.
James M. Lowry, security.

Robert Lemmens, aged 8 years on the 16th of September last past,
bound to David Reed until he attains the age of 21 years. Leeland
Davis, security.

William A. Leming, a minor over the age of 14 years, chose William
S. McGaughey as his guardian. William Cavener, security.

Page 158 Solomon Smith appointed guardian of Jesse C. Moyers, a
minor. Nathaniel S. Moyers, security.

William P. Kelly appointed guardian of Margaret and Joseph Kelly,
minor heirs of David Kelly, decd. William C. McCoy and Joseph
Newberry, securities.

Jacob Myers appointed guardian of Elijah Willoughby, a minor.
John Willoughby, security.

<u>1855 Monday 4th June</u>
  Page 179 It appearing to the satisfaction of the Court that in the
  appointment of Claibourn Self guardian of Mary Jane Casteel and
  others, the name of Richard Casteel is erroreous and ought to be
  Jonathan Casteel.

<u>1855 Monday 2nd July</u>
  Page 189 William Casteel appointed guardian of Sarah Jane and
  Joseph Columbus Susong, minors. Martin Welty, security.

<u>1855 Monday 3rd September</u>
  Page 204 Andrew J. Campbell appointed guardian of Sarah, Elizabeth
  and Alfred Carter, minor heirs of William Carter and Hannah Carter,
  decd. Jacob Myers, security.

  Page 205 John Maltsbarger appointed guardian of Nancy Emaline and
  Rebecca Ann Baseter, minor heirs of James Baseter, decd. David
  Maltsbarger and William Miller, securities.

<u>1855 Tuesday 4th September</u>
  Page 207 Henry Watkins, a free boy of color, aged 9 years, bound to
  Thomas Jackson until he attains the age of 21 years. Andrew J.
  Rhea, security.

<u>1855 Monday 1st October</u>
  Page 209 Martha Creamer appointed guardian of Thomas Russell Creamer
  and Virginia Adeline Creamer, minor heirs of Thomas Creamer, decd.
  John Crabtree esqr., security.

  Samuel H. Kelton appointed guardian of Rebecca H. Kelton, his wife,
  formerly Rebecca H. Evans, a minor. Marshall Hartman, security.

  David Dickson appointed guardian of David, William, Henry and George
  Cutshall, minor heirs of John Cutshall, decd. Barnard Cooter, sec.

  William Ricker appointed guardian of George Cutshall, minor over 14
  years of age, he having chose said William Ricker his guardian.
  Mason K. Jones, security.

  Page 218 Jesse Baseter, a minor over the age of 14 years, chose
  James Shanks as his guardian. John E. Kidwell, security.

<u>1855 Monday 5th November</u>
  Page 223 Jacob Starnes appointed guardian of Louisa Ellen Tadlock,
  minor heir of John Tadlock, decd. Joseph Fraker and David Maltsbarger, securities.

  Page 224 Joseph Fraker appointed guardian of Tennessee Tadlock,
  minor heir of John Tadlock, decd. Jacob Starnes and David Maltsbarger, securities.

  James M. Campbell appointed guardian of Margaret Campbell, a minor.
  Adam P. Campbell and Andrew Logan, securities.

<u>1855 Monday 3rd December</u>
  Page 229 William Pearce appointed guardian of Margaret C., Mary Ann
  and John W. Pearce, minors. John Pearce, security.

<u>1856 Monday 7th January</u>
  Page 234 William F. Fowler, a minor over the age of 14 years, chose
  George M. Spencer his guardian. William Johnson and Walter C.
  Willis, securities.

  James E. Wolaver, a minor over the age of 14 years, chose William
  Ealy as his guardian. William Wolaver, security.

  Page 235 James M. Rader appointed guardian of Jane Summit, Sarah
  Summit, Hannah A. Summit, Daniel Summit, William Rader and Mary Ann
  Rader, minors. Samuel Rader, security.

  James W. Duncah appointed guardian of David Bruce, James Jerome,
  Adaline Jane and Mary Rankin, minor heirs of Robert Rankin, decd.
  Lewis Rankin and David davault, securities.

Smith Sawney, a free boy of color, aged 8 years on the 30th of June last past, bound to John W. Rose until he attains the age of 21 years. William G. Fellers, security.

1856 Monday 4th February
Page 247 Eliza Brown, aged 12 years in July last past, bound to R. A. Crawford until she attains the age of 19 years. Robert Mason, security.

Page 248 James Redenhours, aged 15 years in July last past, bound to George Redenhours until he attains the age of 21 years. Enoch M. Moore, security.

1856 Monday 3rd March
Page 255 Syrena Wolaver, aged 13 years, bound to John A. Mason until she attains the age of 18 years. Robert Mason, security.

Polly Ann Wolaver, aged 12 years on the 18th of May last past, bound to Robert Mason until she attains the age of 18 years. John A. Mason, security.

Isaac Wolaver, aged 15 years on the 1st of August last past, bound to Jeremiah McMillan until he attains the age of 21 years. Peter Harmon of Isaac, security.

1856 Tuesday 4th March
Page 262 Smith Columbus Freshour, alias Smith Sawney, a free boy of color, aged 8 years on the 30th of June last past, bound to William B. Robinson until he attains the age of 21 years. David Scott, security.

1856 Tuesday 8th April
Page 283 Samuel McGaughey appointed guardian of John R. McGaughey, minor heir of Richard W. McGaughey. James P. McDowell, security.

Harriet L. Payne, a minor over the age of 14 years, chose James Britton Sr. as her guardian. James Britton Jr., security.

1856 Monday 5th May
Page 299 Margaret Brown appointed guardian of her own children: Richard Wesley, Wilson Bayles, Martha Elizabeth, William Alexander and James Madison Brown, minor heirs of Peter Brown, decd. Christian Bible and Aaron Bible, securities.

1856 Monday 2nd June
Page 302 Henry Trobaugh, a minor over the age of 14 years, chose Christian Bible as his guardian. B. McDannel, security.

Abraham Naff appointed guardian of Samuel Patten, Sarah Jane and Martha Jane Armstrong, minor heirs of Sophia B. Armstrong, decd. E. F. Mercer, security.

1856 Tuesday 3rd June
Page 304 Dorcas Payne appointed guardian of Nancy and Mary D. Campbell, minor heirs of Nathan and Martha Campbell, decd.

1856 Tuesday 8th July
Page 315 John Hinkle, aged 13 years on the 7th of June last past, bound to Margaret Wren until he attains the age of 21 years. E. C. Cochran, security.

James Heaton, aged 7 years in February last past, bound to Jacob H. Feazel until he attains the age of 21 years. Christian Catron, security.

1856 Monday 4th August
Page 317 George McCulpin, alias Holder, aged 7 years, bound to Jonathan Prather until he attains the age of 21 years. Bales Jones, security.

Thomas Alexander McCulpin alias Holder, aged 10 years, bound to John Brannon until he attains the age of 21 years. Jacob Feezel, security.

Marion Brady, aged 12 years on the 11th of December last past, bound to Elijah W. Headrick until he attains the age of 21 years. Robert E. Johnson, security.

1856 Tuesday 5th August

Page 321 Keziah McCulpin alias Holder, aged 4 years, bound to Charles Jackson until she attains the age of 18 years. C. M. Vestal, security.

1856 Monday 1st September

Page 329 William Heaton, aged 3 years, bound to Alfred Brumley until he attains the age of 21 years. David Brumley, security.

Andrew English (of John) appointed guardian of Martha, John and Eliza Shields, minors. James Williams, security.

1856 Monday 6th October

Page 333 William Everhart, a minor over the age of 14 years, chose Shadrack S. Babb as his guardian. Also appointed guardian of Polly Ann, Daniel, James and Anna Jane Everhart, minor heirs of Nicholas Everhart decd. Jeremiah McMillan, John Malone, James Williams, Henry Smith and Loyd Bullen, securities.

Jacob F. Brooks appointed guardian of Selina P., John T., Elizabeth, Mary C., Abram H., George W. and William E. Brooks, minors. A. W. Howard, security.

Page 334 Joseph E. Charleton, aged 14 years on the 6th of November last past, bound to Joseph Hartman until he attains the age of 21 years. Azor Koontz, security.

Victoria Adalaid Charleton, aged 7 years on the 8th day of September last past, bound to Joseph Hartman until she attains the age of 18 years. Azor Koontz, security.

William Franklin Drayman, aged 4 years on the 14th of November last past, bound to Joseph Nease until he attains the age of 21 years. William Ottinger, security.

1856 Tuesday 7th October

Page 341 John H. Ross appointed guardian of Hannah Jane, Mary Ann, James Harrison, Rebecca Caroline, Lewis Alexander and John Robinson Marsh, minor heirs of James Marsh, decd.

1857 Monday 5th January

Page 372 W. Conway Malone appointed guardian of Daniel R., Sarah J., William, James and Thomas A. Moore, minor heirs of James M. Moore, decd. James Shaw, security.

1857 Tuesday 6th January

Page 374 Franklin Harris, a free boy of color, aged 6 years on the 1st of January 1857, bound to William B. McCord until he attains the age of 21 years. John H. Willis, security.

William A. Carson appointed guardian of Margaret Carson formerly Margaret Smelcer. James Johnson, security.

Page 375 James Johnson appointed guardian of Elizabeth Johnson formerly Elizabeth Smelcer, a minor. William A. Carson, security.

Allen McPheron appointed guardian of Rachel Carter, a minor heir of William C. Carter, decd. W. Cavener and James Britton Jr., sec.

Levi Henshaw appointed guardian of Samuel W., Launy J., Mary C., Rebecca E., Martha L., Margaret V., Sarah R. and Temperance Leming, minor heirs of John Leming, decd. A. W. Howard, Azor Koontz and Philip Henshaw, securities.

Page 382 James A. Galbreath appointed guardian of David R. Jewel, a minor heir of Seburn Jewel, decd. Lewis J. Drake and John R. Moore, securities.

1857 Monday 2nd February

Page 384 James Heaton, aged 7 years in February 1857, bound to Thomas C. Easterly until he attains the age of 21 years. A. J.

Rhea, security.

1857 Tuesday 3rd February
Page 388 Lewis J. Drake appointed guardian of Jane, Andrew J. and William Drake, minor heirs of Jesse J. Drake, decd. Sam Milligan, security.

1857 Monday 2nd March
Page 392 Samuel Parman appointed guardian of Ephraim, Elizabeth and Martha Elen Wilhite, minors. John Gourley and Wylie Kelley, securities.

1857 Tuesday 3rd March
Page 406 Samuel Keller appointed guardian of Alexander, Samuel, Talitha and Joel Carter, minor heirs of Ezekiel Carter, decd. Peter Harmon of Isaac, security.

1857 Monday 6th April
Page 407 Thomas Hughes appointed guardian of Mary Eliza Hughes, minor heir of George Hughes, decd. Abraham Hughes, security.

Gilbert Woolsey appointed guardian of William W., George W., Leephaniah, Sarah J., Ruth A., John L. and Abraham Reynolds, minors. William B. Woolsey, security.

Jacob Harris appointed guardian of George, David, William and Henry Cutshall, minors. William M. Lowry, security.

1857 Wednesday 8th April
Page 422 Henry Trobaugh, a minor over the age of 14 years, chose James Britton Jr. as his guardian. Lewis J. Drake, security.

1857 Monday 4th May
Page 423 Livonia Coggburn, aged 8 years, bound to Henry Ellenburg until she attains the age of 18 years. A. J. Rhea and William D. McLeelland, securities.

1857 Tuesday 5th May
Page 430 Henry Harris, a free boy of color, aged 8 years in February last past, bound to James H. Rumbough until he attains the age of 21 years. J. W. Chockley, security.

1857 Monday 1st June
Page 434 James Frederick Helton, aged 3 years on the 6th of July last past, bound to Daniel Y. Miller until he attains the age of 21 years. George M. D. Parry, security.

Isaac B. Morrison, aged 11 years in October last past, bound to Gabriel Henry until he attains the age of 21 years. John Kidwell, security.

Harmon Kenney appointed guardian of John Rednours, a minor. James Williams, security.

1857 Monday 6th July
Page 446 William A. Henderson appointed guardian of Alfred G. Hale, a minor. Andrew J. Kinser, security.

Jesse Glascock appointed guardian of William Glascock, Mary S. Hale and Elbert S. Hale, minors. Andrew J. Kinser, security.

Page 447 Thomas D. Cavener appointed guardian of George G. C. Cavener, a minor. John Cavener, security.

1857 Monday 7th September
Page 457 John R. Low, a minor over the age of 14 years, chose John McGaughey as his guardian. Samuel McGaughey, security.

1857 Tuesday 8th September
Page 461 Elizabeth Kerbaugh appointed guardian of William W. and Euseba Kerbaugh, minors. Allen T. Johnson, security.

<u>1857 Monday 5th October</u>
Page 468   John Russell appointed guardian of Anna, Jonathan, Catharine,
Susannah and Mary Magdaline Renner, minors. John Bowers, security.

<u>1857 Monday 2nd November</u>
Page 476   James Marion Pinkston, aged 6 years on the 2nd of March
last past, bound to Gabriel Phillips until he attains the age of
21 years. John Willoughby, security.

Page 477   Willet Mahog, a mullatto boy, aged 10 years on the 24th of
December last past, bound to John McGuffin until he attains the age
of 21 years. Jacob Harris, security.

<u>1857 Monday 7th December</u>
Page 486   Sarah M. Woolhaver, aged 2 years on the 6th of June last
past, bound to Elbert M. Rambo until she attains the age of 18 years.
James G. Reeves, security.

James B. Rodgers, a minor over the age of 14 years, chose John Ball
as his guardian. William S. Crouch and Samuel H. Baxter, securities.

Joseph B. Walker appointed guardian of William, James, Samuel and
Caroline R. Allen, minors. Daniel Allen, security.

Page 487   Dorcas Payne appointed guardian of Nancy Elizabeth and
Mary Dorcas Campbell, minors. Thomas Britton Sr., security.

<u>1857 Tuesday 8th December</u>
Page 494   Ella Jane Ellison, aged 5 years in May last past, bound to
Elbert Biggs until she attains the age of 18 years. James Galbreath,
security.

<u>1858 Tuesday 5th January</u>
Page 501   Samuel R. Kennedy appointed guardian of Samuel P., Sarah
Ann and Martha Jane Armstrong, minors. Robert S. Bowman, security.

<u>1858 Wednesday 6th January</u>
Page 512   Nancy A. R. Parman, aged 11 years in September last past,
bound to Robert A. Crawford until she attains the age of 21 years.
James Britton Jr., security.

<u>1858 Tuesday 2nd February</u>
Page 522   Theodore Dennis, aged 4 years on the 1st of October last
past, bound to Samuel Ottinger until he attains the age of 21 years.
James Britton Sr., security.

James H. Marsh, a minor over the age of 14 years, chose William
McCord as his guardian. John Willis, security.

Anderson W. Walker appointed guardian of Sarah Elizabeth, John,
Mary, Andrew, William A., George T. and Susan C. Hawk, minors.
William Shields and Jonathan Easterly, securities.

<u>1858 Monday 5th April</u>
Page 551   John Hawk appointed guardian of John, Sally, Mary, Anna,
William, Thomas and Susan Hawk, minors. Andrew Stine, Henry
Ottinger and Benjamin F. Ball, securities.

Isaac Tunnel appointed guardian of Malinda E. Tunnel, a minor.
James Shanks and Andrew English, securities.

<u>1858 Tuesday 6th April</u>
Page 559   Delila Marsh appointed guardian of Rebecca Caroline, Sevier
Alexander and John Robinson Marsh, minor heirs of James Marsh, decd.
Azor Koontz, Samuel S. Hawkins, William B. McCord, John C. Martin,
James Maloney, William H. Russell and Henry Marsh Jr., securities.

Lingo F. Ripley appointed guardian of Mary A. Ripley, his wife,
formerly Mary A. Marsh, a minor heir of James Marsh, decd. Thomas
Ripley, security.

<u>1858 Monday 3rd May</u>
Page 562   John Rankin appointed guardian of David Bruce, William
Jerome, Mary E. and Adaline J. Rankin, minor heirs of Robert Rankin,

decd. David R. Johnson and Lewis Rankin, securities.

William H. McCoy appointed guardian of Margaret and Joseph Kelley, minors. A. W. Howard, security.

Hester Ann, a girl of color, aged 8 years in August last past, bound to   Henry B. Baker, security.

1858 Monday 7th June
Page 568 Jacob Newberry appointed guardian of Benjamin F. and Isabella Caroline Waddle, minors. William M. Wilhoite, security.

Page 569 Abraham Carter, aged 6 years in June 1858, bound to John C. Hankins until he attains the age of 21 years. A. J. Babb, security.

1858 Monday 5th July
Page 572 Henry Harris, a free boy of color, aged 9 years in February last past, bound to Roswell E. Kingsley until he attains the age of 21 years. James H. Rumbough, security.

1858 Monday 4th October
Page 604 Felix Barnhart appointed guardian of Henry and Barbara Barnhart, minors. Jonathan Prather and Jefferson Gfellers, security.

1858 Tuesday 5th October
Page 609 James G. Crum, aged 11 years on the 11th of October 1858, bound to James G. Reeves until he attains the age of 21 years. J. G. Gass, security.

1858 Monday 1st November
Page 616 William W. Teague, aged 13 years on the 16th of October last past, bound to Ephraim Link until he attains the age of 21 years. Jacob Harris, security.

1859 Monday 3rd January
Page 6 James M. Hunter appointed guardian of Martha L. and Narcissus Hunter, minor heirs of John Hunter, decd. John Willoughby, security.

Alpha Manuel, a free girl of color, aged 10 years on the 15th of March last past, bound to William Johnson until she attains the age of 21 years. Nathan B. Johnson, security.

1859 Monday 7th February
Page 21 Lafayette Dennis, aged 5 years on the 1st of October last past, bound to Henry Harrison until he attains the age of 21 years. James Davis, security.

Page 26 Thomas Jasper Lawson, aged 10 years in September last past, bound to Henry E. Wills until he attains the age of 21 years. A. J. Harmon, security.

George Washington Lawson, aged 10 years in September last past, bound to Alexander J. Harmon until he attains the age of 21 years. Henry E. Wells, security.

Page 27 Joseph Fraker appointed guardian of Louisa Ellen Tadlock, a minor heir of John Tadlock, decd. Thomas Hays and John H. Mullins, securities.

1859 Monday 4th April
Page 34 Jacob Ingle, aged 8 years on the 12th of February last past, bound to Cornelius Hardin until he attains the age of 21 years. William S. McGaughey, security.

Dulciana Dennis, aged 7 years on the 30th of November last past, bound to James A. Broyles until she attains the age of 18 years. A. W. Howard, security.

Alexander Irvin, aged 15 years on the 12th of February last past, bound to Thomas Caldwell until he attains the age of 21 years. William S. White, security.

Page 37 Lemuel K. Cox appointed guardian of William Anderson, a minor. William Gass, security.

Thomas Russell appointed guardian of William Franklin Rader and Elbert Martin Rader, minor heirs of Andrew Rader, decd. James M. Dunwoody, James Mc. Dunwoody, John Dunwoody and John M. Gass, securities.

James A. Broyles appointed guardian of Benjamin F. and Isabella Caroline Waddle, minors over the age of 14 years. Isaac Seaton and John F. Broyles, securities.

1859 Monday 2nd May
Page 48 Hannah Jane McCulpin, aged 8 years in April last past, bound to Richard W. Brown until she attains the age of 18 years. George Kenney, security.

Page 49 James Harmon Houlder, aged 7 years, bound to Charles H. Rite until he attains the age of 21 years. A. W. Howard, security.

William Houlder, aged 5 years, bound to James W. Harold until he attains the age of 21 years. C. H. Rite, security.

1859 Monday 6th June
Page 58 John Hinkle, aged 16 years on the 1st of July 1859, bound to Elizabeth Ren until he attains the age of 21 years. Andrew J. Debusk, security.

Harriet Caroline Hinkle, aged 9 years on the 8th of August last past, bound to Elizabeth Ren until she attains the age of 18 years. A. J. Debusk, security.

1859 Monday 4th July
Page 64 Absalom T. McCulpin, aged 3 years on the 24th of May last past, bound to Smith Alexander until he attains the age of 21 years. Jonathan Prather, security.

John Morrison, aged 3 years on the 5th of April last past, bound to George W. Wolaver until he attains the age of 21 years. William Wolaver and A. J. Rhea, securities.

1859 Tuesday 5th July
Page 70 Wesley Cannon, a free boy of color, aged 14 years, bound to John A. Mason until he attains the age of 21 years. S. G. W. Haynie, security.

1859 Monday 5th September
Page 80 Samuel Pickering appointed guardian of Benjamin Johnson, a minor. David R. Johnson and Adam B. Tullen, security.

Page 81 Robert Henry appointed guardian of James Henry, a minor heir of Thomas C. Henry, decd. A. M. Doak, security.

1859 Monday 3rd October
Page 87 J. H. Smith appointed guardian of Thomas J. and John Smith, minors. Isaac D. Smith and Isaac Jackson, securities.

John Weems appointed guardian of James Alison Weems and John Alexander Weems, minors. James C. Weems and Elijah K. Weems, securities.

Page 91 James R. Bailey appointed guardian of William R., Matilda Catharine, Narcissa Felora and Elizabeth Ann Bailey, minors. John G. Weems, security.

Page 92 William C. Meney appointed guardian of Granville J. Glascock, a minor. John Shields and Isaac D. Smith, securities.

William C. Maloney appointed guardian of Susannah L. Glascock, a minor. John Maloney and T. D. Cavener, securities.

Page 95 William M. Easterly appointed guardian of Susan Easterly, formerly Susan Evans, a minor. Jacob Easterly, security.

1859 Tuesday 4th October
    Page 103 George Russell, a free boy of color, aged 16 years, bound
    to Robert C. Carter until he attains the age of 21 years. E. F.
    Mercer, security.

1859 Monday 5th December
    Page 112 Mary McMackin appointed guardian of Louisa Elizabeth and
    Martin V. B. McMackin, minors. Thomas Brumley, security.

    Orpha Horton appointed guardian of William J., James K. P., John
    and ? S. Horton, minors. James Coulter, Stephen Huff and
    Warren H. Horton, securities.

1860 Monday 6th February
    Page 132 Christian Bowers appointed guardian of Reuben, Lydia,
    Leander, James, Susan and Martha Bowers, minors. A. Susong,
    security.

    Page 133 Philip Lonas appointed guardian of Catharine E. Johnson,
    George A. Lonas, Henry W. Lonas, James D. Lonas and Margaret
    Elizabeth Lonas, minors. Philip Johnson, Absalom Lonas, John
    Johnson and S. J. Johnson, securities.

    William C. Maloney appointed guardian of Emily, John W., William
    C., Laura Ellen and James Brown, minors. Loyd Bullen and Leeland
    Davis, securities.

1860 Monday 5th March
    Page 146 Nathan B. Johnson appointed guardian of John A., Joseph B.
    and William H. Johnson, minors. Hugh Brown, security.

    Reuben H. Davis appointed guardian of Hester Isabella Boyd, a minor.
    John S. Love, security.

    Thomas S. Gable appointed guardian of Catharine N. Gable, a minor.
    Hiram Gable, security.

    Page 148 James S. McConley, a minor aged 11 years on the 4th of
    January last past, bound to James C. Weems until he attains the
    age of 21 years. William Justice, security.

1860 Monday 7th May
    Page 206 John Wesley Crum, a minor over the age of 14 years, chose
    Rufus K. Waddle as his guardian. William Houston and Eli F. Rambo,
    securities.

    John Morrison, aged 4 years on the 5th of April last past, bound to
    Robert Literal until he attains the age of 21 years. James H.
    Hogan and James Shaw, securities.

    Page 207 William Riley, a boy of color, aged 5 years, bound to
    Alfred Brumley until he attains the age of 21 years. William
    Wolaver, security.

    Henry Feezel, aged 8 years, bound to Nancy Ann Feezel until he
    attains the age of 21 years. John Brannon, security.

1860 Monday 4th June
    Page 225 Daniel Britton appointed guardian of James M. Reed, a
    minor. George W. Gray and Charles G. Rankin, securities.

1860 Tuesday 3rd July
    Page 244 Mary Harris, aged 7 years in October last past, bound to
    Henry Guggenheimor until she attains the age of 18 years. R. A.
    Crawford, security.

1860 Monday 6th August
    Page 246 John Hull appointed guardian of Isaac B. and Samuel Hull,
    minors. Daniel D. Hull, security.

    Reece Porter Scruggs, a minor over the age of 14 years, chose Jacob
    W. Harrison as his guardian. James Harrison, security.

    Allen McPheron appointed guardian of Andrew J. and William G. Drake,
    minors. James Britton Jr., security.

1860 Monday 3rd September

Page 259 Andrew S. Freshour appointed guardian of James Crum, a minor. Lewis Click and William Crum, securities.

William Hawkins appointed guardian of Thomas D., Jacob and Elizabeth Williams, minors. John B. Hawkins, security.

1860 Monday 1st October

Page 268 John Parman appointed guardian of Catharine Winkle, a minor. William Crum and Robert A. Crawford, securities.

Rufus K. Waddle appointed guardian of William Crum, a minor heir of John Crum, decd. Hiram T. Price, Joseph P. Jane and George Click, securities.

Page 270 Newton McDonald Lawson, aged 15 years on the 14th of April last past, bound to Michael George until he attains the age of 21 years. Thomas N. Brooks, security.

Daniel N. Salts, aged 7 years on the 1st of October 1860, bound to William H. Britton until he attains the age of 21 years. Daniel Britton, security.

1860 Tuesday 2nd October

Page 277 Ephraim Davis appointed guardian of Oliver P. Starnes, a minor. George M. Spencer, security.

James A. Galbreath appointed guardian of David R. Jewel, a minor heir of Seburn Jewel, decd. H. G. Robertson and James Jones, securities.

1860 Monday 5th November

Page 280 Elbert Hale appointed guardian of Mary S. Hale, a minor. Isaac Jackson and Alfred G. Hale, securities.

Joseph Powell appointed guardian of Mary and Charles Rabe, minor heirs of Doctr. Charles Rabe, decd. R. L. Rabe and James H. Rumbough, securities.

William Dugger appointed guardian of Sarah Duggar, John Duggar, Elizabeth Duggar and Hyla Malone?, minors. John Justice, security.

1860 Monday 3rd December

Page 289 Jacob England, aged 8 years, bound to Hugh Carter until he attains the age of 21 years. Cornelius Hardin, security.

Thomas Heaton, aged 5 years, bound to J. C. Brumley until he attains the age of 21 years. David Brumley, security.

Page 291 Benson M. Bailey appointed guardian of William, Tilghman A., and Elizabeth Florence Bailey, minors. Wyly Campbell, security.

Philip B. Bird appointed guardian of Cornelius Porter Fillers, Albert Lytel Fillers and John Fillers, minors. Matthias Bird, security.

1861 Monday 4th February

Page 315 John Johnson, aged 4 years in August last past, bound to George G. Britton until he attains the age of 21 years. Daniel Britton, security.

Elizabeth Smith, aged 10 years in June last past, bound to Edward Hendry until she attains the age of 18 years. William Hendry, security.

William W. Easterly appointed guardian of Theodrick Evans, a minor. V. S. Lotspeich, security.

1861 Monday 4th March

Page 319 Robert Hardin Ragsdale, aged 4 years on the 17th of January last past, bound to Samuel A. Crozier until he attains the age of 21 years. William Hendry, security.

<u>1861 Monday 1st April</u>
Page 329 William Johnson appointed guardian of Alexander, William
H. and Joseph Johnson, minor heirs of Nathan B. Johnson, decd.
Loyd Bullen and William S. Oliphant, securities.

<u>1861 Tuesday 2nd April</u>
Page 336 Mary E. Parrott appointed guardian of George M. Parrott,
a minor. John J. Mitchell, security.

<u>1861 Monday 6th May</u>
Page 342 Isaac Cannon, a boy of color, aged 13 years in August last
past, bound to John A. Mason until he attains the age of 21 years.
Joshua C. Lane, security.

John Squibb appointed guardian of Sarah C., Mary J., Barton,
Caroline and William B. Stanfield, minors. George E. A. Smith,
security.

<u>1861 Monday 3rd June</u>
Page 353 Samuel R. Kennedy appointed guardian of Samuel P. Sarah
Ann and Martha Jane Armstrong, minors. Thomas Hays and Robert C.
Gray, securities.

<u>1861 Monday 1st July</u>
Page 358 Spencer A. Ball appointed guardian of Elizabeth Josephine
Strong, a minor. James Murphey, security.

Page 360 Mary Ann Wolaver appointed guardian of David A., Nancy
and Tolbert Susong, minors. David Cook, security.

<u>1861 Monday 2nd September</u>
Page 381 George Morrison, aged 6 years, bound to Thomas Russell
until he attains the age of 21 years. Alfred Brumley, security.

Henry Waterford, a free boy of color, aged 20 years on this day,
bound to J. C. Hankins until he attains the age of 21 years.
Jacob Myers, security.

<u>1861 Tuesday 3rd September</u>
Page 385 William Britton appointed guardian of Jane R., Thomas,
William Bruce and David Britton, minors. James Britton Jr., sec.

<u>1861 Monday 7th October</u>
Page 388 William Benson, aged 5 years, bound to E. S. Murphey until
he attains the age of 21 years. John G. Reeves, security.

Oscar Henry, a free boy of color, aged 17 years on the 14th of
October last past, bound to C. M. Vestal until he attains the age
of 21 years. Robert C. Carter, security.

Page 389 Calvin Mathes, a free boy of color, aged 16 years on the
1st of May 1861, bound to James Creamer until he attains the age of
21 years. Azor Koontz, security.

Harriet Shannon, a free girl of color, aged 13 years, bound to
William K. Vance until she attains the age of 21 years. David
G. Vance, security.

<u>1861 Tuesday 8th October</u>
Page 392 George Manual, a free boy of color, aged 19 years, bound
to Thomas J. Murphey until he attains the age of 21 years. Thomas
Lane, security.

<u>1861 Monday 4th November</u>
Page 394 John Cavener, aged 8 years on the 23rd of May last past,
bound to William Cavener until he attains the age of 21 years.
John Maloney, security.

Page 395 Loyd Jackson appointed guardian of Alexander, Mary Ann,
Richard C. and James P. Jackson, minor heirs of John T. Jackson,
decd. James Johnson and James T. Jackson, securities.

<u>1861 Tuesday 5th November</u>
Page 400 Mary Adelaide Coleman, a free girl of color, aged 8 years
on the 14th of March last past, bound to Thomas D. Arnold until she
attains the age of 21 years. Cornelius Hardin, security.

Scyntha Ann Coleman, a free girl of color, aged 5 years on the 16th
of March last past, bound to Thomas D. Arnold until she attains the
age of 21 years. Cornelius Hardin, security.

Henry Montgomery Coleman, a free boy of color, born on the 10th of
January last past, bound to T. D. Arnold until he attains the age
of 21 years. Cornelius Hardin, security.

<u>1861 Monday 2nd December</u>
Page 401 Clary Henry, a free girl of color, aged 6 years, bound to
J. C. Brumley until she attains the age of 21 years. Alfred Brumley,
security.

Caleb Harrison appointed guardian of Amos J., David B., Jacob F.,
William A. and Simon B. Harrison, minors. Henry A. Farnsworth,
security.

<u>1862 Monday 6th January</u>
Page 404 James Mason appointed guardian of Matilda and William
Mason, minor heirs of Robert Mason, decd. John A. Mason and Joseph
Mason, securities.

Page 407 William Warrick, a free boy of color, aged 14 years on the
15th of July last past, bound to Ebenezer Morrow until he attains
the age of 21 years. James Britton Jr., security.

<u>1862 Monday 3rd February</u>
Page 417 William Alexander Brown, aged 13 years on the 10th of
April last past, bound to George B. Simpson until he attains the
age of 21 years. John W. Byerly, security.

<u>1862 Wednesday 5th March</u>
Page 432 Isaac A. Allen appointed guardian of Mary Ruth, Earnest
and Martha C. Allen, minors. William M. Lowry, security.

<u>1862 Monday 7th April</u>
Page 454 Alexander McLin appointed guardian of Benjamin McLin, a
minor. Philip Harmon, security.

William P. Hankins appointed guardian of Sarah Margaret Hankins, a
minor. John E. Kidwell and Henry M. Hankins, security.

Abraham S. Johnson appointed guardian of Keturah, Angeline, Mary
Ann and Jane Pickering, minors. Samuel Pickering and Daniel
Britton, securities.

Page 460 John McAlister, aged 7 years in October last past, bound
to Adam P. Campbell until he attains the age of 21 years. Robert
A. Crawford, security.

<u>1862 Monday 5th May</u>
Page 471 Daniel Everhart and James Everhart, minors over the age of
14 years, chose Alfred Couch as their guardian. William Ross, sec.

<u>1862 Monday 2nd June</u>
Page 478 William Milburn appointed guardian of Bratt? Warford
Fraker, William Elbert Milburn Fraker, Malinda Caroline Fraker
and Michael Brabson Fraker, minors. Harmon Kenney, security.

Azor Koontz appointed guardian of John and Martha Spencer, minors.
Archibald M. Reeser, security.

<u>1862 Tuesday 3rd June</u>
Page 482 Harriet Showman, a free girl of color, aged 14 years,
bound to James H. Fleming until she attains the age of 21 years.
S. P. Crawford, security.

46

1862 Monday 7th July

Page 491 Robert Magee, aged 9 years, bound to George Creamer until he attains the age of 21 years. Azor Koontz, security.

Lewis Richard Simpson, aged 4 years on the 2nd of June last past, bound to John A. Ross until he attains the age of 21 years. William McAmis, security.

Page 492 Isaac Murray appointed guardian of Matilda and John Bayles, minor heirs of Luke Bayles, decd. A. M. Reeser and John F. Broyles, securities.

1862 Monday 1st September

Page 506 Elkanah Harris, a free boy of color, aged 10 years on the 5th of September 1862, bound to Ebenezer Morrow until he attains the age of 21 years. William Morrow, security.

Page 507 John Rader appointed guardian of Daniel, William, James and Samuel Rader, minors. John Burkey and James M. Dunwoody, securities.

1862 Monday 6th October

Page 513 Josiah A. Peninoh, aged 12 years on the 10th of August last past, bound to Thomas Hays until he attains the age of 21 years. James Shanks, security.

James Walker, aged 14 years on the 15th of September 1862, bound to Thomas Thomason until he attains the age of 21 years. Lewis Rankin, security.

John Deputy, aged 7 years, and James Franklin Deputy, aged 4, bound to Daniel Beals until they attain the age of 21 years. Lewis Rankin, security.

1862 Monday 3rd November

Page 524 Moses Evans, aged 7 years, bound to William S. Oliphant until he attains the age of 21 years. Jacob McNeese, security.

1862 Monday 1st December

Page 525 Martha Fillers, aged 2 years, bound to Henry Wagner until she attains the age of 18 years. William M. Lowry, security.

Richard Evans, aged 4 years, bound to Gabriel Henry until he attains the age of 21 years. William M. McAmis, security.

Page 526 Margaret Ripley appointed guardian of Virginia V. and Bloomfield W. Ripley, minor heirs of Thomas Ripley, decd. Elbert S. Ripley and John Squibb, securities.

1863 Monday 5th January

Page 533 Anderson Magee, aged 7 years, bound to James O. Hoyol until he attains the age of 21 years. William McAmis, security.

William Magee, aged 11 years, bound to John D. Carson until he attains the age of 21 years. Solomon Harmon, security.

1863 Monday 2nd February

Page 539 James V. Heaton, aged 13 years on the 10th of February 1863, bound to William H. Russell until he attains the age of 21 years. James M. Lowry, security.

1863 Monday 2nd March

Page 543 William C. Maloney appointed guardian of Daniel R., Sarah Jane, William, James and Thomas A. Moore, minor heirs of James M. Moore, decd. Thomas J. Easterly and Loyd Bullen, securities.

1863 Monday 4th May

Page 556 Alexander Laughlin appointed guardian of Margaret Elizabeth Laughlin, a minor. William Cavener, security.

1863 Monday 6th July

Page 562 Mary Ann Mitchell, aged 12 years on the 21st of July 1863, bound to Jacob A. Hacker until she attains the age of 18 years. S. P. Crawford, security.

John D. Shackleford, aged 9 years on the 19th of May last past, bound to James Henry until he attains the age of 21 years. Andrew Bradford, security.

Adaline Shackleford, aged 7 years in February last past, bound to James Henry until she attains the age of 18 years. Andrew Bradford, security.

William Guthrie appointed guardian of Mahala Domaro?, a minor. John McGuffin, security.

1863 Monday 6th July
Page 565 Eliza L. Kennedy appointed guardian of Samuel Patten Armstrong, Sarah Ann Armstrong and Martha Jane Armstrong, minors. Thomas Hays Sr. and Robert C. Gray, securities.

1863 Monday 3rd August
Page 568 George Dinsmore, aged 5 years in June last past, bound to George Hannah until he attains the age of 21 years. John F. Broyles, security.

1863 Monday 7th September
Page 578 W. F. Reeser appointed guardian of Andrew Crawford Fraker, a minor. John Crabtree, security.

Page 579 William Ellis appointed guardian of Elizabeth V. and William Henry Nichols, minors. Thomas Chedister, security.

1863 Monday 2nd November
Page 582 John Ashley, aged 11 years, bound to James C. Ervin until he attains the age of 21 years. William B. Rankin, security.

1864 Monday 1st February
Page 592 Mitchell Shackleford, aged 4 years, bound to James Evans until he attains the age of 21 years. Andrew Bradford, security.

1864 Monday 4th April
Page 1 Matilda Hollans, aged 9 years, bound to David Brumley until she attains the age of 18 years. Henry A. Farnsworth, security.

1864 Monday 5th September
Page 17 Lee Walker, aged 10 years on the 17th of September 1864, bound to Samuel Lane until he attains the age of 21 years. William S. White, security.

1865 Monday 3rd April
Page 26 Asbury H. Jones, appointed guardian of Nancy Catharine Jones and George Russell Jones, minor heirs of Margaret Jane Jones.

1865 Monday 5th June
Page 61 William Dinsmore, appointed guardian of Penelope F. Dinsmore, a minor. James Harrison, security.

Margaret Hartman appointed guardian of Sarah E. Hartman, a minor. Henry J. Hartman, security.

Joseph Mathews appointed guardian of Marsel H., Solomon A., Martha Jane and Franklin L. Mathews, minors. Henry J. Hartman and William Pettit, securities.

Isaac Smelser appointed guardian of Henry Jackson Smelser, John W., William A., Margaret E., James F., Barbara J. and Isaac V. Smelser, minors. A. D. Susong, security.

1865 Tuesday 6th June
Page 64 Peter Myers appointed guardian of George M. Simpson, a minor. Henry Simpson and William Reed, securities.

1865 Wednesday 7th June
Page 65 Walter C. Willis appointed guardian of John Horton and Juliet S. Horton, minor heirs of Joseph Horton, decd. James C. Wilson, security.

<u>1865 Monday 3rd July</u>
Page 79 William Pierce appointed guardian of Rebecca Jane Redenhour,
a minor. William Ellis, security.

<u>1865 Monday 4th September</u>
Page 110 David Ellis appointed guardian of Nancy Ann, Elizabeth,
Rebecca Jane and Matilda Ellis, minors. William Ellis and Nathan
B. Smith, securities.

<u>1865 Monday 2nd October</u>
Page 124 John C. Rambo appointed guardian of John A. Broyles, a
minor. William Cavener, security.

Elihu McNeese appointed guardian of Mary Jane, Martha M., Samuel
H., Joseph H. and John J. C. McNeese, minors. Samuel McNeese,
security.

Page 125 Andrew McMackin appointed guardian of William, Levi,
Andrew M. and Juriah? Isabel Harrison, minors. William McMackin
and Elburt S. Smith, securities.

<u>1865 Monday 6th November</u>
Page 139 Olivia P. Starnes appointed guardian of P. Starnes,
William C., George A., Ephraim D., Nancy F. and Thomas A. Starnes.
Ephraim Davis and John Starnes, securities.

Page 140 Cathrine Miles appointed guardian of Jane and William A.
Miles, minors. Jacob Keicher and Isaac Bibble, securities.

Andrew Susong appointed guardian of Margaret Oregon, William,
John, David C. and Martha E. Susong, minors. Alexander Susong,
security.

<u>1865 Monday 4th December</u>
Page 164 Joseph Swatzell, aged 10 years on the 9th of December
present, bound to James C. Ervin until he attains the age of 21
years. H. C. Smith, security.

William C. Campbell, aged 7 years on the 22nd of May last past,
bound to James Wright until he attains the age of 21 years. John
Wright, security.

Page 167 A. W. Howard appointed guardian of Margaret, Mary Ann and
John Pierce, minors. Joseph P. Jane and Rufus K. Waddle, securities.

James R. Day appointed guardian of Ruth Day, a minor. John Day,
security.

Martha Sexton appointed guardian of James J., Joseph A., John F.
and Margaret L. Sexton, minors. Andrew L. Harrold, security.

<u>1866 Monday 1st January</u>
Page 187 Isaac R. Earnest appointed guardian of Mary Virginia
Earnest, a minor. Charles S. Earnest, security.

Page 188 John C. Dyer appointed guardian of Mary Elizabeth, George
W. and Eldridge Solomon Scott, minor children of James C. Scott,
decd. Joseph Mathews, security.

A. S. Johnson appointed guardian of David Bruce, James Jerome,
Mary E. and Adaline Rankin, minors. Jefferson GFellers, Joseph
P. Jane and William Johnson, security.

Page 189 John A. Starnes appointed guardian to William, George A.,
Ephraim D., Nancy F. and Thomas A. Starnes, minors. Oliver P.
Starnes and Ephraim Davis, securities.

Richard Alexander Allen, aged 4 years on the 8th of February next,
bound to James W. Carter until he attains the age of 21 years.
J. B. Hawkins, security.

Jacob England, aged 13 years in February last past, bound to
William Henry until he attains the age of 21 years. J. B. Hawkins,
security.

1866 Monday 2nd January
     Page 190 John A. Swatzell, aged 12 years on the 30th of October
     last past, bound to Charles Lovett until he attains the age of 21
     years. Charles A. Lovett, security.

     Jacob Swatzell, aged 14 years on the 21st of February last past,
     bound to Charles A. Lovett until he attains the age of 21 years.
     Charles Lovett, security.

1866 Monday 5th February
     Page 212 John Bitner appointed guardian of Isaac E., James B.,
     Samuel C. and Brunette Earnest. A. M. Reeser and William Johnson,
     securities.

1866 Monday 2nd April
     Page 263 Joseph Bly Swaney, aged 4 years in July last past, bound
     to John Winkle until he attains the age of 21 years. William Crum,
     security.

1866 Friday 6th April
     Page 276 Joseph B. Dobson appointed guardian of Laura, Isabella and
     Joseph Alexander, minors. John H. Willis, security.

     Thomas T. Robinson appointed guardian of S. W., M. V., S. R. and
     T. C. Leming, minors. M. D. Robinson and John H. Willis, security.

1866 Monday 7th May
     Page 285 William Bible appointed guardian of Joseph M. and Thomas
     M. Bible, minors. Isaac Bible, Thomas J. Easterly and Allen Baker,
     securities.

     Page 286 Barbara Jane Trobaugh appointed guardian of Mary Jane and
     Susan Trobaugh, minors. Christian Bible, security.

     Andrew Johnson Smith, aged 17 years on the 6th of October last
     past, bound to William F. Brown until he attains the age of 21
     years. A. H. Jones, security.

1866 Tuesday 8th May
     Page 292 Samuel H. Babb appointed guardian of George Valentine and
     Hezekiah Balch Babb, minors. John F. Gass and Henry M. Hawkins,
     securities.

1866 Monday 4th June
     Page 307 Elizabeth Pickering, aged 6 years on the 3rd of September
     last past, bound to Jonathan Beals until she attains the age of 18
     years. Nathaniel Pickering, security.

     John E. Myers, aged 14 years on the 20th of April last past, bound
     to Lewis B. Ball until he attains the age of 21 years. James
     Shanks, security.

     Allen English appointed guardian of Richard R. and James P. Jackson.
     A. H. Pierce, security.

     Jesse Collett appointed guardian of Mary Caladena and William W.
     Collett, minors. John Crabtree, security.

1866 Monday 2nd July
     Page 313 William Duggar appointed guardian of John and Elizabeth
     Duggar, minors. George W. Gass, security.

     David S. Hays appointed guardian of Thomas E. Hays, a minor. John
     Hays and A. J. Marshall, securities.

     John D. McMillan appointed guardian of Margaret A. E. and Sarah R.
     Fox, minor heirs of Jacob Fox, decd. J. C. Lane and J. G. Gass,
     securities.

     Catharine Jackson appointed guardian of Darthewly and Thomas
     Jackson, minors. G. C. Pangle and Thomas J. Lane, securities.

1866 Monday 6th August
Page 326   W. A. McKeehan appointed guardian of John W. Aikin, Mary
Eakin and Delia Eakin, minors.   Hiram D. Fraker and E. S. Ripley,
securities.

Fethias Woolsey appointed guardian of Jackson and Marion Smith,
minors. David Rush, security.

1866 Tuesday 7th August
Page 334   David Fry appointed guardian of George W. Dunbar, a minor.
D. G. Vance and Robert M. Salts, securities.

1866 Monday 3rd September
Page 337   William White appointed guardian of Rachel, Deborah and
Elijah Coulson, minors. Mary Coulson and Joseph White, securities.

Page 344   Nathaniel Pickering appointed guardian of Rebecca S.
Pickering, a minor. George W. Moore, security.

Page 345   David N. Cloyd appointed guardian of Jacob S. Farner, a
minor heir of Jacob Farner, decd. William Myers, security.

William Ross appointed guardian of James Albert Jones, a minor.
George Kenny, security.

1866 Tuesday 4th September
Page 350   David Fry appointed guardian of W. P., Mary M. C., Marcella
J. and Matilda B. Hunt, minors. R. M. Saltz, J. M. Gass and J. G.
Gass, securities.

1866 Monday 1st October
Page 361   Rufus Jones, aged 12 years, bound to Samuel Bruner until
he attains the age of 21 years. John B. Hawk, security.

Page 362   Deadrick A. Fulkes, aged 12 years, bound to N. B. Westmoreland until he attains the age of 21 years. David Barham, sec.

Page 363   Augustus B. Fulkes, aged 14, bound to N. B. Westmoreland
until he attains the age of 21 years. David Barham, security.

1866 Monday 5th November
Page 377   William M. Campbell appointed guardian of Sarah Jane
Setters?, Martha An Campbell and Samuel M. Russell, minors. Alfred
Susong and Hezekiah Smith, securities.

Page 378   Mary E. Gooden, aged 6 years on the 12th of January last
past, bound to William A. Brown until she attains the age of 18
years. J. B. Hawkins and Claiburn Wibb, securities.

Andrew J. Baker, aged 4 years in March last past, bound to William
H. McCoy until he attains the age of 21 years. Sparling Bowman,
security.

1866 Monday 3rd December
Page 391   Nicholas N. Fulkes, aged 8 years, bound to N. B. Westmoreland until he attains the age of 21 years. R. M. Salts, security.

1867 Monday 7th January
Page 403   David Byerly appointed guardian of Ida Emma Florence,
Frank F., Ann Mary and David F. Byerly, minors. Jesse R. Earnest,
security.

Page 407   Valentine S. Rader appointed guardian of Harriet Courtney
Franklin Rader, Sena E. Rader and James H. Rader, minors. William
Rader, security.

David Presnell appointed guardian of Sarah E., John, Lucinda C.,
M. Henry, Andrew J. and Nancy A. Arrowood, minors. James Wilburn
and Aaron Archer, securities.

Page 408   Jacob Hays appointed guardian of Barnet and Hail Baxter,
minors. S. H. Baxter and David Rush, securities.

William S. White appointed guardian of Nancy M. M., Thomas R. M.
and Francis Manen Baxter. Jacob Hays, security.

1867 Monday 4th February

Page 417 Hannah M. Sexton appointed guardian of William M., Thomas F., Sarah C., Mary D., Joseph H., John H. and James H. Sexton, minors. Hugh E. Cotter, security.

Mary Jane Reynolds, aged 8 years, and Margaret Reynolds, aged 6 years, bound to Lewis Gentry until they attain the age of 18 years. William Gentry, security. (Elizabeth Gentry, wife of Lewis Gentry, was mother of Mary Jane and Margaret. S.K.H.)

Page 418 James D. Wykle appointed guardian of Henry Carter Feezel, a minor. Alfred Susong, security.

A. W. Jane appointed guardian of Charles Pierce, a minor. Joseph P. Jane and William Johnson, securities.

1867 Monday 5th March

Page 433 Thomas Davis appointed guardian of George, Thomas L., Charles and Jane McAmis, minors. Thomas Loyd, security.

Page 434 William A. Small, aged 12 years on the 6th of June last past, bound to William V. Lewis until he attains the age of 21 years. N. B. Smith and James M. Brown, securities.

Allen English appointed guardian of Norris B., Elizabeth and Mary English, minors. Andrew English, security.

William A. Fraker appointed guardian of Andrew C. Fraker, a minor. George W. Fraker and Charles Loyd, securities.

Isaac M. Swaney appointed guardian of George W. W. and James Swaney, minors. Andrew English and A. H. Pierce, securities.

1867 Tuesday 2nd April

Page 467 James Carter, aged 12 years on the 1st of June last past, bound to George M. Spencer until he attains the age of 21 years. John A. Brown, security.

Samuel H. Baxter appointed guardian of A. G. R. Baxter, a minor. David Rush, security.

1867 Monday 6th May

Page 471 Thomas Hays appointed guardian of Martha Amanda, Isaac Bowman and Harriet Jane Hays, minors. David Fry, security.

John Wright appointed guardian of John L., Florence and Laura Courtney. James M. Trobaugh and George J. Courtney, securities.

1867 Monday 3rd June

Page 493 Elizabeth Johnson appointed guardian of Richard Hucks, a minor. John Johnson, security.

1867 Monday 1st July

Page 505 Thomas Nease appointed guardian of Jacob Harvey and John M. Nease, minor children of John Nease, decd. A. W. Walker, sec.

Emaline Russell appointed guardian of Margaret Clemmentine, Sarah Virginia and Ann Elizabeth Russell, minors. Samuel Cochran, sec.

John Susong, aged 8 years, bound to Alfred Susong until he attains the age of 21 years. James Susong, security.

1867 Monday 5th August

Page 524 Henry B. Baker appointed guardian of David F. Baker Jr. A. W. Walker, security.

James Allen appointed guardian of Daniel Earnest Allen and Martha T. Allen, minors. Jacob McNeese, security.

Page 532 Gabriel Henry appointed guardian of Phebe Catharine, Sarah Alice, Mary Elizabeth and Lydia Jane Crumley, minors. John B. Hawkins, security.

Page 533 James O. Earnest appointed guardian of Sarah Jane and David Lewis Earnest, minors. Harvey W. Earnest, security.

<u>1867 Monday 2nd September</u>
Page 543 Martha M. Good appointed guardian of William David, Mary Ann Elizabeth and Elbert Hastrell Good, minors. Charles Loyd, security.

Page 546 John S. Richardson, aged 10 years on the 1st of June last past, bound to Isaac Crawford until he attains the age of 21 years. Nathan Morelock, security.

Page 547 William S. White appointed guardian of Mary Isabella, Virginia P., Margaret Jane and John Logan Stuart, minors. James B. Rodgers, security.

Henry A. Farnsworth appointed guardian of Jose Shepherd, a minor. Joseph A. Farnsworth, security.

<u>1867 Monday 7th October</u>
Page 564 R. C. Myers appointed guardian of William, John, Daniel, James and Vina Ricker, minor heirs of Nancy Ricker, decd. Samuel L. Stephens, security.

George B. Muncher appointed guardian of Eliza Ann, John, Oliver, Melvina and Mary Caroline Muncher, minors. William H. McCoy, security.

George B. Muncher appointed guardian of Nancy Ann and Catharine Blake, minors. William H. McCoy and George Click, securities.

Page 565 William Weems appointed guardian of William A., Mary Jane and Nancy Elizabeth Crumley, minors. Thomas N. Weems, security.

Page 566 James M. Allen appointed guardian of Martha Ann Allen, a minor. Oliver Holt and George L. Porter, securities.

William Sutters appointed guardian of Sarah Sutters, a minor. Oliver Holt and George L. Porter, securities.

<u>1867 Monday 4th November</u>
Page 574 Thomas E. Hays, aged 5 years on the 26th of October last past, bound to Joseph Newberry until he attains the age of 21 years. Sparling Bowman, security.

Page 577 John Sexton appointed guardian of Harriet Sexton, formerly Harriet Cogburn. David W. Mercer and Christian Bible, securities.

<u>1867 Monday 2nd December</u>
Page 589 Joseph R. Huntsman appointed guardian of Joseph O., Nancy E., George W., Eleanor J. and Jane P. Lane, minor heirs of A. J. Lane, decd. John S. Dyer, A. P. Haun, Enoch Marshall and Thomas J. Dean, securities.

Nathaniel Pickering appointed guardian of Mary and Rebecca Syrena Pickering, minors. John N. Bright, security.

Page 599 John Keller, a boy of color, aged 14 years, bound to Samuel Keller until he attains the age of 21 years. John Keller, security.

Betsey Keller, a girl of color, aged 12 years, bound to Samuel Keller until she attains the age of 21 years. John Keller, sec.

Madison Rader appointed guardian of William Franklin Rader, a minor over the age of 14 years. John A. Reed, Marshall Hartman and Jacob M. Myers, security.

Catharin Brown appointed guardian of John Strother Brown, a minor child of Joseph Brown, decd. D. D. Hull, security.

<u>1867 Saturday 7th December</u>
Page 607 John Williams, aged 1 year, bound to Warren Williams until he attains the age of 21 years. V. S. Maloney, security.

<u>1868 Monday 6th January</u>
Page 617 Alexander W. Carter appointed guardian of Samuel, Joel M., and Telitha Carter, minors. George Lady and Matilda Carter, sec.

53

Page 619 Anderson W. Walker appointed guardian of Laura W. P., Mary M. C., Marcella J. and Matilda B. Hunt, minors. Henry B. Baker, security.

Page 622 John E. Hendry appointed guardian of Clarissa, James C. and Cornelius Carter, minors. Cornelius Hardin, security.

George W. Campbell appointed guardian of Samuel Russell, a minor. Madison Rader, security.

1868 Monday 3rd February
Page 623 Jacob W. Reeser appointed guardian of Adaline Virginia Reeser, formerly Adaline Virginia Creamer. W. F. Reeser, security.

Page 631 Daniel Simpson appointed guardian of George M. Simpson, a minor. Peter Myers, security.

H. C. Harmon appointed guardian of Amanda A. and Mary Jane Harmon, minors. John Harmon, security.

1868 Monday 6th April
Page 12 William R. Rodgers, a minor over the age of 14 years, chose Wylie Campbell as his guardian. James M. White, security.

Alfred Marshall appointed guardian of Sarah Ann Brown, a minor. Abner Babb, security.

Rufus Jones, aged 12 years, bound to Cornelius Smith until he attains the age of 21 years. A. Smith, security.

Page 18 Solomon Matthews appointed guardian of Catharine J., Eliza C., Mary C., William and Sarah A. Trobaugh, minors of John Trobaugh, decd. James S. Stroud and J. B. Hurley, securities.

Sarah Jane Jones, aged 6 years on the 4th of February 1868, bound to Lewis Anderson until she attains the age of 18 years. E. M. Moore, security.

1868 Tuesday 7th April
Page 22 John E. Hendry appointed guardian of Massa Jane, Angela, John E. and Alfred Brown, minor children of John H. Brown, decd. John R. Sayler and Heston Cox, securities.

1868 Saturday 11th April
Page 26 Richard W. Brown appointed guardian of William D., Masa Jane, Sarah Ann, John E. and Alfred Brown, minors. Alfred Marshall, security.

1868 Monday 4th May
Page 34 Jane Boyd appointed guardian of Gemima E., James B., Juliett M. and Emma C. Ingle, minors. Elbert S. Murphey, security.

Page 35 William Henry appointed guardian of Wilson McAmis, Joseph McAmis, Sarah McAmis and Margaret Delitha Henry, minors. Gabriel Henry, security.

Allen Anderson appointed guardian of John Casteel, a minor. William Ross (of Allen), security.

1868 Tuesday 5th May
Page 37 Margaret Irwin appointed guardian of Eliza and Jenny Bele Irwin, minors. Robert M. McKee, security.

1868 Monday 1st June
Page 48 Leander Bowers appointed guardian of James, Susan and Jane Bowers, minors. H. C. Smith and James Henry, securities.

James C. Irwin appointed guardian of Susan, Jacob, Andrew and Emiline Swatzel, minors. W. C. Scruggs, security.

George T. Weems appointed guardian of Elizabeth J. Weems, a minor. R. B. Weems, security.

Page 49 Samuel R. Reeve, aged 10 years, bound to John C. Dyer until he attains the age of 21 years. James Visage, security.

1868 Monday 6th July
Page 59 Margaret Brandan appointed guardian of Lydia Ann, Lucinda, Martha A. and James H. McClary, minors. A. H. Pierce, security.

W. C. Willis appointed guardian of Lamantine, Mantraville, Victor and Jutilla McMillan, minors. David M. Dobson, security.

Jacob Haun appointed guardian of Margaret Cantrey, a minor. Solomon Matthews and James S. Straud, securities.

James W. Cloyd appointed guardian of J. S. Farner, a minor. George Hartman, security.

Page 60 William S. Ricker, aged 2 years on the 28th of January last past, bound to William J. Ruble until he attains the age of 21 years. Sparling Bowman, security.

1868 Monday 1st August
Page 67 John Redenours appointed guardian of Nancy C., Edward G. and John A. Redenours, minor children of John Redenours and Sarah Jane Redenours. Lazrus Redenours, security.

1868 Monday 7th September
Page 72 Jessee Hays appointed guardian of Mary Alice Humphries, a minor. Michael Bright Jr., security.

Page 73 Martha A. Gass appointed guardian of Thomas N., John B. and George B. King, minors. William Stoncifer, security.

1868 Tuesday 8th September
Page 79 A. W. Miller appointed guardian of Martha, James and Nancy E. Basinger, minors. H. B. Baker, security.

1868 Monday 5th October
Page 90 Sarah Bradley appointed guardian of Malvina, Thomas, Newton and Elizabeth Brandan, minor children of Endimman and Sarah Brandan. Alexander H. Pierce, security.

Page 92 William Walker appointed guardian of Martha J. Armstrong, a minor. S. H. Baxter and Solomon Miller, securities.

James R. Day appointed guardian of James Day, a minor heir of Andrew J. Day. John Day, security.

1868 Tuesday 6th October
Page 97 Alpheus Doty appointed guardian of William and James Peters, minor heirs of Samuel Peters, decd. And Hester A. Britton, Jacob R. Peters, Samuel D. Peters, John N. Peters and Emeline R. Peters, minor heirs of F. W. Peters, decd. John Peters, security.

Newton Carroll Harrington, aged 10 years on the 7th of February last past, bound to W. A. T. J. Butler until he attains the age of 21 years. Isaac C. Dobson, security.

1868 Monday 2nd November
Page 100 Thomas Neece appointed guardian of Nancy Mariah, Mary Elizabeth, James Isaac and William Houston, minor heirs of James Houston, decd. A. W. Walker, security.

Page 101 Thomas Malone appointed guardian of Mary Jane, William Alexander and Nancy Elizabeth Crumley, minor children of William Crumley and Rebecca Crumley, decd. John Malone Esqr., security.

Daniel Rader appointed guardian of James Rader, a minor. James Davis Esqr., security.

1868 Tuesday 3rd November
Page 104 John E. Collet appointed guardian of Mary C. Collet, a minor child of William Collet, decd. Hiram Remine, security.

Maunney Farnsworth, aged 12 years on the 18th of August last past, and Elliet Farnsworth, aged 9 years last past, and Jason Farnsworth, aged about 7 years, bound to Henry A. Farnsworth until they attain the age of 21 years. William Johnson, security.

Maunney Spinkle, aged 10 years on the 13th of August last past 1868, and Charles W. Spinkle, aged 7 years on the 23rd of May last past 1868, bound to David S. Ripley until they attain the age of 21 years. O. B. Headrick, security.

1868 Monday 7th December

Page 105 Solomon Matthews appointed guardian of Thomas Matthews, a minor. H. T. McMillan, security.

Page 106 James Wright appointed guardian of Joel H., Jacob C. and William G. Campbell, minor heirs of William H. Campbell, decd. John Wright, security.

N. O. Henry appointed guardian of John and James Henry, minor heirs of Robert Henry, decd. N. M. Henry, security.

Page 107 William Walker appointed guardian of Sarah A. Walker, formerly Sarah A. Armstrong. John B. Walker, security.

1869 Monday 4th January

Page 117 James Wright appointed guardian of David S., William G., Joel H. and Jacob C. Campbell, minor children of William C. Campbell, decd. John Wright, security.

John Casteel appointed guardian of Robert and William Smith, minors. William Casteel, security.

Page 118 James Pruet, aged 4 years, bound to Andrew O. Susong until he attains the age of 21 years. H. C. Smith, security.

1869 Tuesday 5th January

Page 128 Martha Pruet, aged 8 years on the 3rd of May last past, bound to Levi Woods until she attains the age of 18 years. A. W. Walker, security.

1869 Monday 1st February

Page 136 W. E. V. Jackson appointed guardian of David J. Baker, a minor heir of David F. Baker. Samuel D. McPheron, Peter R. Rader, John A. Rader and Augustine H. Arnett, securities.

1869 Monday 1st March

Page 155 Charles Collet appointed guardian of Alice Collet, a minor. William A. Browning, security.

L. K. Tolifer appointed guardian of Margaret Ann, James B. and George M. Tunnel, minors. Allen English, security.

Alexander Brown appointed guardian of David A., Samuel L., Mary E. J., James F., Andrew J. and Gilbert F. Babb, minors. Seth Babb, security.

1869 Monday 5th April

Page 163 L. C. Ramsey appointed guardian of Alexander, S. D. and W. F. Ramsey, minors. M. S. Doak, her security.

1869 Tuesday 6th April

Page 182 Anderson W. Walker appointed guardian of McHenry, Andrew J., and Nancy A. Arrowood, minor children of William Arrowood, decd. Robert M. McKee, security.

1869 Monday 3rd May

Page 193 Isaac Easterly appointed guardian of Raten F. and Alexander W. Justis, minors. F. M. Easterly, security.

1869 Monday 7th June

Page 208 Matilda E. Mason and William J. Mason, minors 14 years of age, children of Robert Mason, decd., chose Isabella Ewit as their guardian. Margaret Erwin, security.

Page 209 B. D. Harold appointed guardian of Hannah E. Webb, a minor. W. Hawkins, security.

Page 211 A. E. Susong appointed guardian of George A., Ephraim D., Nancy F. and Thomas A. Starnes, minors. Anderson Susong, security.

Martha A. Thompson appointed guardian of Mary E., James D., Margaret J. and George A. Graham, minors. E. M. Moore, security.

John McCurry appointed guardian of John and Robert Kelley, minors. George Gass, security.

1869 Monday 5th July

Page 218 Isaac Dearstone appointed guardian of Leza Bele, Martha Oliva and James Alexander Sevier, minor children of Alexander A. Sevier, decd. John D. Hybarger, William Russell and H. C. Smith, securities.

S. S. Babb appointed guardian of Martha Ann Fowler, a minor. M. V. Brown, security.

1869 Tuesday 6th July

Page 222 Mary Ann Fitzgerald, a minor over the age of 14 years, chose for herself and Maggie, Thomas and Elizabeth Fitzgerald, J. C. Brumley as their guardian. James A. Galbreath, security. (Children of Anna Fitzgerald, decd. - S.K.H.)

1869 Monday 2nd August

Page 236 Henry Wilson, aged 17 years in March last past, bound to Nathan B. Smith until he attains the age of 21 years. John Squibb, security.

E. M. Moore appointed guardian of Edward, Peter and Mary Doud, minor heirs of Patrick Doud, decd. James H. Chedister, security.

Page 239 Joseph W. Mattacks, aged 9 years on the 22nd of July last past, bound to Leander Bowers until he attains the age of 21 years. J. C. Ervin, security.

Wilson B. Johnson appointed guardian of George A. and Eliza C. Johnson, minors. Wyley Campbell, security.

1869 Wednesday 8th September

Page 260 William B. Brown appointed guardian of Eliza, Sarah and Andrew Stover, minor heirs of Daniel Stover, decd. David S. Ripley, security.

1869 Monday 4th October

Page 266 Henderson Linch appointed guardian of Josephine, Franklin Taylor and George Houston Linch, minors. Azor Koontz, security.

1869 Tuesday 5th October

Page 274 Silva E. Jones, aged 13 years, bound to J. C. Brumley until she attains the age of 18 years. A. J. Gass, security.

1869 Wednesday 6th October

Page 278 J. L. Taylor appointed guardian of William A. and Ellender C. Crum, minor heirs of Emanuel Crum and Mary E. Crum. C. M. Willis, security.

1869 Monday 1st November

Page 282 John Barlow appointed guardian of Elizabeth and Sarah Willoughby, minors. John T. Myers, security.

E. M. Moore appointed guardian of Elizabeth, Tempy, Jane, James and George Graham. William Ross (of Allen), security.

William Ross (of Allen) appointed guardian of Mary Ann, Maggie, Thomas and Elizabeth Fitzgerald, minors. E. M. Moore, security.

Levi Harrison, aged 15 years on the 20th of June last past, bound to Washington A. Lemons until he attains the age of 21 years. O. B. Headrick, security.

Page 284 E. M. Moore appointed guardian of Granville T. Evans, a minor child of John Evans, decd. William Ross (of Allen), sec.

1869 Monday 6th December

Page 295 Thomas Lane Sr. appointed guardian of James A. and Rosa Lane, minor heirs of Henry? Magile, decd. Thomas Lane Jr., sec.

Page 296 George W. Bowman appointed guardian of Martha Ellen Bowman, a minor. Thomas Shaw, security.

1870 Tuesday 4th January
Page 315 Malinda A. Winters appointed guardian of Sarah Elizabeth Winters, a minor. George W. Hensley, security.

Page 316 On motion and it appearing to the satisfaction of the Worshipful County Court of Greene County, that Malinda A. Winters is the Mother of a minor child, Sarah E. Winters, and that William P. Winters, Father of the said Sarah E. Winters and husband of the said Malinda A. Winters, has abandoned her the said Malinda A. Winters without any lawful cause.

1870 Monday 7th February
Page 323 John Courtney appointed guardian of Rhoda C. and William T. Courtney, minors. Saymour Haun, security.

William Courtney appointed guardian of James N. and Madison L. Courtney, minors. Adam Haun, security.

Page 324 Andrew N. Harrison, aged 12 years in October last past, bound to James F. Kirk until he attains the age of 21 years. James Jones, security.

Page 325 John Jennings appointed guardian to James, Robert, Mary Catharine, Mahulda and Thomas Blake, minors. George Jennings, security.

1870 Monday 7th March
Page 337 John Armitage appointed guardian of George Armitage, a minor heir of Alfred Armitage, decd. E. F. Mercer, security.

1870 Monday 4th April
Page 361 William S. McGaughey appointed guardian of John R. McGaughey, a minor. Thomas Alexander, security.

W. W. Harris appointed guardian of B. F., William, M. B. and Malinda C. Fraker, minors. Charles Loyd and Cornelius Mays, security.

1870 Monday 2nd May
Page 376 Mary Catharine Bright and Jacob Bright, minor over the age of 14 years, chose William S. White as their guardian. M. C. Bright, security.

Isham English, colored, appointed guardian of Franklin English, colored, a minor. J. H. Chedister, security.

Page 377 John Grant, aged 3 years, bound to Susannah Varner until he attains the age of 21 years. William Johnson, security.

1870 Monday 6th June
Page 398 A. J. Ludmilk, aged 5 years in April last past, bound to P. T. Woodward until he attains the age of 21 years. N. B. Smith, security.

Noah Mayfield, aged 12 years on the 14th of September last past, bound to Barbara Huff until he attains the age of 21 years. H. C. Smith, security.

A. N. Haun appointed guardian of Isaac M. Horton and Martha Horton, minors. E. M. Moore, security.

Page 399 William Carlton, aged 4 years on the 15th of November last past, bound to A. S. Freshour until he attains the age of 21 years. M. C. Williams, security.

1870 Tuesday 7th June
Page 401 Walter C. Willis appointed guardian of St. Ignatius Hevius Wyrick, a minor. A. W. Walker, security.

1870 Tuesday 5th July
Page 408 B. W. Fraker, a minor over the age of 14 years, chose William Milburn as his guardian. H. D. Fraker, security.

W. F. Reser appointed guardian of Sarah Catharine Smith, a minor. John Squibb, security.

Franklin Morelock, aged 9 years on the 24th of December last past, bound to Jerry A. Morelock until he attains the age of 21 years. James Keebler, security.

Page 409 John Johnson, aged 2 years on the 25th of December last past, bound to William T. Clem until he attains the age of 21 years. A. W. Walker, security.

1870 Monday 5th September

Page 441 Felix A. Reeve appointed guardian of Anzula Buxton, a minor. E. W. Headrick, security.

William Johnson appointed guardian of Morgan N. and Charles G. Johnson, minors. James B. Gauntt, security.

1870 Tuesday 6th September

Page 459 William B. Seaton appointed guardian of Mary A., Sarah E., and Charles S. Nelson, minor heirs of William R. Nelson, decd. Barton Seaton, security.

1870 Monday 3rd October

Page 468 Sarah Gfellers appointed guardian of Ann Gfellers, a minor. Lewis H. Broyles, security.

William P. Brown appointed guardian of Harriet L., Ellener and Peter G. Brown, minors. William M. Ferguson, security.

Page 469 S. S. Babb appointed guardian of Martha J. and George J. Redenour, minor children of James Redenour, decd. James Luster, security.

1870 Monday 7th November

Page 480 Peter Meyers appointed guardian of U. S. Grant Meyers, William Shearman Meyers and John Meyers, minors. Christopher Meyers, security.

William M. Grace appointed guardian of Louisa, Samuel and Elbert Dunlap, minors. A. H. Pettibone, security.

Page 481 Peter Ball appointed guardian of William C. Elder, a minor heir of William R. Elder, decd. William R. Ellison, security.

1870 Monday 5th December

Page 503 Amanda Jane Collett appointed guardian of John L. and Robert L. Crabtree, minor heirs of Barney Crabtree, decd. Lloyd Bullen, security.

1871 Tuesday 3rd January

Page 511 Robert M. McKee appointed guardian of Ruthy Day, a minor child of Andrew J. Day, decd. Samuel E. Snapp, security.

Lewis M. Haun appointed guardian of Mary, Rebecca Jane and Sarah Wells, minor children of William W. Wells, decd. E. M. Moore, H. C. Harmon and George Rednours, securities.

Page 512 James H. Hogan appointed guardian of Adam M., Sarah E., Mary A., Nancy C. and Joseph R. Dunwoody, minors. William M. Ferguson, security.

1871 Monday 6th February

Page 524 James L. Woods, aged 10 years on the 13th of March last past, bound to J. W. Dearstone until he attains the age of 21 years. A. Brumley, security.

Joacim Bible appointed guardian of Solen A. and Mary A. Bible, minor children of Joacim Bible, Leeland Davis, security.

Sarah Jane Dison?, aged 3 years in November last pased, bound to Thomas Gibson until she attains the age of 18 years. S. L. Stephens, security.

Page 525 B. F. Harrison appointed guardian of George F., Henry C., Mary J. and Rachel C. Harrison, minors. Samuel D. Winters, sec.

1871 Wednesday 8th March
Page 543 Lewis F. Self appointed guardian of Mary Ann, Maggie, Elizabeth and Thomas Fitzgerald, minors. William S. McGaughey, security.

1871 Monday 3rd April
Page 553 George Evans, aged 13 years in September last pased, bound to John H. Renner until he attains the age of 21 years. George Lintz, security.

Jonathan Bible appointed guardian of Charles L. and Barbara E. Bible, minor children of James Bible, decd., and his wife Nancy Bible. Leeland Davis, security.

Page 554 William Ross (of Allen) appointed guardian of Mary Ann Malaru?, a minor. A. W. Walker, security.

Page 555 C. M. Vestal appointed guardian of Annie, Elizabeth, Maggie and Thomas Fitzgerald, minors. Samuel L. Stephens, sec.

A. E. Ripley appointed guardian of Idaho and David S. Ripley, minors. W. F. Reser and William R. Brown, securities.

Page 556 J. B. Hensley appointed guardian of Mary Ann, Alexander and Harriet P. Wisecarver, minors. Zacariah Hensley, C. P. Williams, and John Lynch, securities.

Hennley S. Maloney appointed guardian of James A. Scruggs, a minor. William C. Maloney and H. D. Maloney, securities.

1871 Tuesday 4th April
Page 563 Isaac B. Gray appointed guardian of Margaret Ann Hawkins, a minor child of Jacob Hawkins, decd. Abner Babb and Rebecca Ross, securities.

1871 Monday 5th June
Page 581 Lizza Dinsmore appointed guardian of Penelope F. Dinsmore, a minor. David Parman, security.

Elizabeth Earnest appointed guardian of Isaac E., James B., Samuel T. and Brunett P. Earnest, minors. John Bitner and B. F. Earnest, securities.

1871 Monday 7th August
Page 598 Christian Bible appointed guardian of William Meisinger, a minor brother of James Meisinger, decd. John Meisinger, sec.

Page 600 Jacob Hawkins appointed guardian of A. J. and Epps Starnes, minors. Nathaniel Smith, security.

1871 Monday 4th September
Page 609 Oliver Holt appointed guardian of William H. C., Mary J., Idelia L. and John D. Wilson, minor heirs of Nathaniel Wilson, decd. Samuel Holt, security.

Oliver Holt appointed guardian of Jacob J., Margaret J., Sarah and E. Holt, minor heirs of Jonas Holt, decd. Samuel Holt, security.

Page 610 Elizabeth Smith appointed guardian of Mary Isabella Coggins, a minor. William K. Smith, security.

1871 Monday 2nd October
Page 616 David R. Gass appointed guardian of Jane Dunwoody, a minor. Daniel Smith, security.

Daniel Smith appointed guardian of Sarah Dunwoody, a minor. David R. Gass, security.

Page 617 William B. Rush appointed guardian of Virginia C., Ruth E. and Florence C. Rush, minor children of William B. Rush. James A. Galbreath, security.

1871 Tuesday 3rd October
    Page 627 Hiram D. Fraker appointed guardian of Mary J., Laura E.,
    Julia C. and Samuel H. McInturff, minor children of Christopher
    McInturff, decd. A. W. Walker, security.

1871 Monday 6th November
    Page 9 Elizabeth Blakely and Henry Blakely appointed guardians of
    Mary Ann Malone, a minor child of Smith H. Malone, decd. A. W.
    Walker, security.

    Rebecca L. Brown appointed guardian of Mary and Charles P. Robe,
    minor children of Charles Robe, decd. John A. Brown, security.

    Page 10 Frederick Scruggs appointed guardian of William D. McCurry,
    a minor heir of John D. McCurry. William C. Scruggs, security.

    A. W. Walker appointed guardian of Elizabeth, Nancy Ann and James
    F. Griffith, minor heirs of Stephen Griffith, decd. H. C. Harmon,
    security.

1871 Monday 4th December
    Page 21 J. R. C. Painter appointed guardian of Sidney C., Lacy L.
    and Clyde E. Lawrence, minors. F. W. Lawrence and James W. Coleman,
    securities.

    Page 22 Fethias Woolsey appointed guardian of Elizabeth, Lucinda,
    Keziah, M. A. S., Grinsfield L., Jensie L. and Minnie S. Woolsey,
    minor children of Israel Woolsey, decd. Alexander M. Smith, sec.

1872 Monday 1st January
    Page 33 James Deputy, aged 13 years, bound to W. J. Dodd until he
    attains the age of 21 years. William S. McGaughey and James
    Oliphant, securities.

    John Deputy, aged 16 years, bound to Marion W. Brooks until he
    attains the age of 21 years. B. F. Harrison, security.

1872 Tuesday 2nd January
    Page 43 George W. Forsinger, aged 5 years on the 26th of January
    last past, bound to Henry Dicks until he attains the age of 21
    years. George Clem, security.

1872 Monday 4th March
    Page 65 George A. Bacon appointed guardian of Jacob A., Thomas and
    Charles F. Bacon, minor children of Enoch Bacon, decd. Jacob
    Hybarger, security.

    Page 66 Thomas Maloney appointed guardian of James Scruggs, a minor.
    William C. Maloney, security.

    Elijah Hayes, aged 11 years, bound to Joseph Newberry until he
    attains the age of 21 years. Elias Newberry, security.

    Page 67 M. H. Whillock appointed guardian of Orlena Moody, a minor
    child of Benjamin Moody, decd. James Collett, security.

    N. Cobble appointed guardian of Adam M., Sarah E., Mary J., Nancy
    C. and Joseph R. Dunwoody, minor children of Joseph R. Dunwoody,
    decd. H. C. Smith, security.

1872 Monday 1st April
    Page 86 George W. Scott, a minor over the age of 14 years, chose
    John C. Dyer as his guardian. Jeremiah McMillan, security.

    A. J. Frazier appointed guardian of David, Samuel, Mary E., James,
    Andrew J., Gilbert and Leander Babb. James B. Gauntt, security.

    Page 87 Harvey W. Earnest appointed guardian of Asuba Britton, a
    minor child of James H. Britton, decd. James O. Earnest, security.

    Franklin English, aged 10 years on the 25th of December last past,
    bound to Isam English until he attains the age of 21 years. D. F.
    Marshall, security.

    Page 91 Robert S. Browning appointed guardian of William H. C.,
    Mary J. Idelia L. and John D. Wilson, minor children of Nathaniel

Wilson, decd. Eli Rader, security.

1872 Tuesday 2nd April
Page 92 James Fry appointed guardian of Elizabeth, Nancy Ann and
James Griffith, minor children of Stephen Griffith, decd. David
Fry and Catharine Fry, securities.

1872 Monday 6th May
Page 97 Henry D. McNite appointed guardian of Catharine Jane McNite,
a minor. Anthony McNite, security.

Page 100 William Hawkins appointed guardian of Mahala Florence
Strong, a minor child of Hiram A. Strong, decd. James Linebaugh,
security.

1872 Tuesday 7th May
Page 104 R. H. M. Donnelly appointed guardian of Mary J., Laura E.,
Julia C., Samuel H. and Mahala E. McInturff, minor children of
Christopher McInturff, decd. Hiram D. Fraker, security.

S. W. Swofford appointed guardian of Joseph D. McLelland, a minor
child of William D. McLelland, decd. Joseph B. Dobson, security.

1872 Monday 3rd June
Page 109 John A. Weems appointed guardian of William D. Brown, a
minor child of Jotham Brown, decd. B. D. Harold, security.

1872 Tuesday 4th June
Page 110 A. W. Walker appointed guardian of Nancy A. and James F.
Griffith, minor heirs of Stephen Griffith, decd. O. B. Headrick,
security.

1872 Tuesday 2nd July
Page 121 Thomas Law appointed guardian of McHenry, Andrew J. and
Nancy A. Arrowood, minor children of William Arrowood, decd.
A. W. Walker, security.

William S. White appointed guardian of Nannie C., William P.,
Mallie J. and Benjamin L. Quinn, minors. James Shanks, security.

1872 Monday 5th August
Page 124 Albert Ford appointed guardian of Caroline Stanfield, a
minor. John W. Ellis, security.

Susan Foster, colored, bound to Adam Morrow until she attains the
age of 18 years. Ebenezer Morrow, security.

Page 125 Alexander M. Smith appointed guardian of Nancy E. Rhea,
a minor child of Alfred F. Rhea, decd. Cornelius Mays and Elbert
S. Murphey, security.

Page 126 Robert S. Browning appointed guardian of Harriet R., John
J. H. and Elbert P. Dunlap, minor children of William Dunlap, decd.
Daniel C. Cooper, security.

1872 Monday 2nd September
Page 162 Charlie W. Sprinkle, aged 12 years on the 23rd of May last
past, bound to H. E. Wells until he attains the age of 21 years.
A. J. Harmon, security.

Page 164 William Henry appointed guardian of Phebe C., Sarah A.,
Mary E. and Lydia J. Crumley, minor children of A. W. Crumley,
decd. Gabriel Henry, security.

1872 Monday 7th October
Page 185 Richard Basket appointed guardian of Mary Coggins, a minor
child of Joshua Coggins, decd. John W. Basket, security.

1872 Tuesday 8th October
Page 192 A. W. Walker appointed guardian of Mark, Alexander, John
and Elizabeth Bayless, minor children of Andrew Bayless, decd.
H. B. Baker, security.

1872 Monday 4th November
        Page 200 Joseph R. Davis appointed guardian of Phebe C. Davis,
        formerly Phebe C. Crumley, a minor. John M. Malone, security.

        H.K. Haworth appointed guardian of George S. Bowers, a minor.
        Mary A. Bowers, security.

1872 Monday 2nd December
        Page 204 Robert M. McKee appointed guardian of Sarah E. and Mary
        J. Bowman, minor children of Sparling Bowman, decd. George B.
        McGaughey, security.

        William W. Easterly appointed guardian of Belle Effie, L.W., John
        S. and Rome Easterly, minor children of the said William W.
        Easterly. J.P. Easterly, security.

        Samuel H. Crawford appointed guardian of James F., Margaret L.,
        William R., and Martha T. McCoy, minor children of Calvin McCoy,
        decd. J.D. McMillan, security.

        Page 205 Abraham Rader appointed guardian of Martha J. Linebarger,
        a minor child of Charles B. Linebarger, decd. Jacob Kiker, sec.

1873 Monday 6th January
        Page 215 Enoch P. Murray appointed guardian of Jacob A. Bewley, a
        minor child of John Bewley, decd. V.S. Murray, security.

1873 Tuesday 7th January
        Page 222 W.F. Green appointed guardian of Horace Hunter, a minor.
        O.B. Headrick, security.

1873 Monday 3rd February
        Page 226 Ozy B. Williamson appointed guardian of Florence Fox,
        widow of Samuel P. Fox, decd. and Carah P. Fox, a minor child of
        said Samuel P. Fox, decd. Isam A. Williamson, security.

        Page 227 Isam A. Williamson appointed guardian of Elizabeth E.,
        John A., Jeremiah C., William J. and Harvey V. Williamson, minor
        children of the said Isam A. Williamson. Ozy B. Williamson and
        Nelson S. Broyles, securities.

        Page 228 Josiah Blazer, aged 5 years on the 1st day of April last
        past, bound to William Blazer until he attains the age of 21 years.
        A.W. Walker, security.

        A.W. Walker appointed guardian of Mary Ann Malone, a minor child of
        Smith H. Malone, decd. O.B. Headrick, security.

1873 Monday 3rd March
        Page 242 Elbert M. Jones appointed guardian of Martha S., John K.,
        Florence, G.L.M. and Mary J. Jones, minors. James Jones and M.S.
        Broyles, securities.

1873 Monday 7th April
        Page 256 Kittie A. Byerly appointed guardian of Ida M.F., Frank F.,
        Ann M. and John D.F. Byerly, minors. Jesse R. Earnest, security.

        Page 258 Joseph Hendry appointed guardian of Richard West, James W.
        Hendry, Nancy C. Hendry and Mary Hendry. Young Carter, security.

        Andrew Fincher, aged 11 years in January last past, bound to B.M.
        Stephens until he attains the age of 21 years. George Pickering,
        security.

        Page 259 William Carter, aged 7 years on the 26th day of January
        last past, bound to James R. Harmon until he attains the age of 21
        years. A.J. Harmon, security.

        Mary A. Holt appointed guardian of Jacob J., Margaret J. and Sarah
        E. Holt, minor children of Jonas Holt (of Jesse). John A. Park,
        security.

        On motion, it is ordered that the Clerk of this Court and he is
        directed to correct the names in a former order of this Court
        appointing Jonathan Bible, guardian of the minor children of
        James Bible, decd., by inserting the names Charles L. Bible,

instead of James L. Bible, and Barbara E. Bible, instead of Bettie E. Bible.

1873 Tuesday 8th April
Page 263   Charles Robinson, aged 5 years, bound to Sithie Morris until he attains the age of 21 years. Rufus Vance, security.

1873 Monday 5th May
Page 272   James Salts appointed guardian of Sarah K. Salts, formerly Sarah K. Smith, a minor. Robert Smith and Allen Salts, sec.

Page 273   M. Gfillers appointed guardian of Florence Gfillers and John A. Gfillers, minors. James Jones, security.

John Harrold appointed guardian of Charles and Jesse Harrold, minors. James Jones and Joseph G. Gass, securities.

1873 Monday 2nd June
Page 279   M.S. Doak appointed guardian of Mary C. Doak, a minor. Samuel S. Doak, security.

1873 Monday 4th August
Page 290   David W. Mercer appointed guardian of Nancy, James and Elizabeth Anderson, minor children of John M. Anderson, decd. Christian Bible, security.

Page 291   Rachel E. Mitchell appointed guardian of Margaret J., Mary A., Tennessee, Robert L., Viola, Flora C. and Emma V. Martin, minors. Robert Mitchell and J.Z.A. Remine, securities.

1873 Tuesday 5th August
Page 300   Thomas Loyd appointed guardian of Margaret E.V. Loyd, a minor. Charles Loyd, security.

1873 Monday 1st September
Page 309   Isham A. Williamson appointed guardian of Florence and Cara Fox, minors. Nelson S. Broyles and Jason W. Williamson, sec.

Page 311   John E. Hendry appointed guardian of Margaret A. and Rachel L.M. Hendry, minors. S.S. Babb, security.

William Pettit appointed guardian of Elizabeth Ann Haun, a minor child of John Haun, decd. Jacob Myers Esqr., security.

Page 312   John Chapman appointed guardian of James B., Fannie and George Chapman, minor children of Mary Chapman, decd. E.E. Bebber and James B. Gauntt, securities.

W.W. George appointed guardian of Joseph M., William and Elizabeth George, minors. Thomas N. Brooks, security.

1873 Monday 3rd November
Page 344   Charles Henegar, aged 9 years on the 10th day of April last past, bound to Richard Gammon until he attains the age of 21 years. William Gammon, security.

John A. Moyers appointed guardian of Sarah M. and John Moyers, minors. William Moyers, security.

1873 Monday 1st December
Page 360   Gideon Burkhart appointed guardian of Rachel E. and Thomas W.R. Gibson, minor children of Thomas Gibson, decd. Charles H. Marsh and George E. Jones, securities.

1874 Monday 5th January
Page 378   Catharine Lamb appointed guardian of Eliza A., William M.P., Nathan W.S., Sarah E. Lamb and Charlotte C. Dill, minors. R.K. Waddle, security.

Page 379   Othneil Bruner appointed guardian of Gilbert N. Bruner, a minor. J.B. Hawkins Esqr., security.

1874 Tuesday 6th January
Page 388   Aulden Tucker appointed guardian of Margaret Brubaker, a

minor. S.S. Babb, security.

<u>1874 Monday 2nd February</u>
Page 395 George W. Cox, aged 8 years on the 5th day of June last
past, bound to Thomas Davis until he attains the age of 21 years.
E.M. Moore, security.

<u>1874 Monday 2nd March</u>
Page 411 A.J. Neas appointed guardian of James F. Neas, a minor.
Jacob Neas, security.

Page 412 Robert Lister appointed guardian of Mary Alice Lister, a
minor. Alfred Brumley, security.

Page 413 James Justice appointed guardian of Sarah E. and Mary J.
Bowman, minor children of Sparling Bowman, decd. Loyd Bullen,
security.

<u>1874 Monday 6th April</u>
Page 421 Charles L. Beatz appointed guardian of R.W. Jones, a
minor. William Neas, security.

Jackson Gfellers appointed guardian of Virginia Ann Fellers, minor.
O.M. Broyles, security.

<u>1874 Tuesday 7th April</u>
Page 432 Millie Bell, aged 4 years on the 15th day of October last
past, bound to Charles Arnold until she attains the age of 18 years.
Jackson Arter, security.

<u>1874 Monday 4th May</u>
Page 437 William Milburn appointed guardian of William M., Martha
E. and Alex. B. Fraker, minor children of D.F. Fraker, decd. A.W.
Walker, security.

Charles Pratt, aged 15 years on the 8th day of May last past,
bound to Reuben Caldwell until he attains the age of 21 years.
Thomas R. McCollum, security.

<u>1874 Monday 1st June</u>
Page 455 John A. Senaker appointed guardian of Frances O., Eliza-
beth J., William D., Neppie S. and Catharine J. Senaker, minors.
M.S. Doak, security.

<u>1874 Monday 6th July</u>
Page 475 Sarah Elizabeth Seaton appointed guardian of Joseph
Franklin and Mary Alice Seaton, minors. Josiah Holt, security.

<u>1874 Tuesday 4th August</u>
Page 497 Thomas Fitzgerald, a minor over the age of 14 years,
chose David Mauman? as his guardian. Patrick Marshall, security.

<u>1874 Monday 7th September</u>
Page 531 William Johnson appointed guardian of Margaret McGee, a
minor child of Philip McGee, decd. J.Z.A. Remine, security.

Page 532 Joseph Dykes appointed guardian of William E. Dykes, a
minor. Jasper Dykes and Jacob Hays, securities.

<u>1874 Monday 5th October</u>
Page 550 Henry Malony, aged 14 years in March last past, bound to
David Bible until he attains the age of 21 years. Thomas J.
Easterly, security.

Sevier Maloney, aged 4 years in June last past, bound to David
Bible until he attains the age of 21 years. Thomas J. Easterly,
Security.

Page 552 Enoch M. Saylor appointed guardian of Mary Ann and Godfrey
E. Saylor, minors. Samuel Linebaugh and Thomas W. Phillips, sec.

<u>1874 Monday 2nd November</u>
Page 560 Jacob Mathews appointed guardian of John, Harriett and

Thomas Mathews, minors. George Mathews and James Strowed, sec.

Francis M. Easterly, aged 7 years in November last past, bound to James M. Saulsbury until he attains the age of 21 years. T.W. Phillips and Gabriel Phillips, securities.

H.S. Borden appointed guardian of James Moody, a minor. James Evans, security.

1874 Monday 7th December
Page 577 William Verran appointed guardian of Thomas and Mary Jane Verran, minors. M.G. Waddle, security.

1875 Monday 4th January
Page 8 Ozy R. Broyles appointed guardian of Barbara R. Broyles, a minor. George B. Park, security.

Page 11 John Burkey appointed guardian of Nancy, Thomas, Virginia and Wilber Burkey, minors. J.R.C. Painter, security.

1875 Monday 1st February
Page 30 William L. Mitchell appointed guardian of Mattie P. Mitchell and Franklen B. Mitchell, minors. D.C. Dukes and J.C. Gass, securities.

James A. Piper appointed guardian of Fannie B., Albert M. and John M. Piper, minors. William L. Mitchell, security.

1875 Monday 5th April
Page 69 Emily G. McCorkle appointed guardian of Nanniebelle and William A. McCorkle, minors. W.H. Moffett, security.

Page 70 Sarah Dyer appointed guardian of E.S. Scott, a minor child of James C. Scott, decd. B.L. Marshall and John Wright, sec.

Page 77 John M. Malone appointed guardian of Lucinda J. and Nancy A. Malone, minor children of Joseph Malone, decd. J.E. Justice Esqr. and James B. Gauntt Esqr., securities.

Page 79 William Smith, aged 16 years on the 10th day of August last past, bound to Henry S. Morelock until he attains the age of 21 years. J.F. Self, security.

1875 Tuesday 6th April
Page 82 John D. McCurly appointed guardian of Kate, Sallie, Alexander, Charles, Hugh and Alice McCurly, minor children of John D. McCurly. E. Willhoit, security.

1875 Monday 3rd May
Page 96 Samuel Malone appointed guardian of Mary Ann Malone, a minor child of Smith H. Malone, decd. John M. Malone and John Malone, securities.

1875 Tuesday 4th May
Page 99 Solomon Reed appointed guardian of James M., John, Mary E. and William D. Reed, minor children of the said Solomon Reed. Leeland Davis, security.

1875 Monday 7th June
Page 112 W.W. George appointed guardian of Penelope F. Dinsmor, a minor. Thomas H. Brooks, security.

1875 Tuesday 8th June
Page 118 Vasta Etter appointed guardian of Franklin, Mollie and Lavina Etter, minors. P.K. Bible, security.

1875 Monday 5th July
Page 124 William H. Hunter? appointed guardian of Mark, Alexander, John and Betty Bayless, minor children of Andrew Bayless, col., decd. C.G. Rankin, security.

Page 125 David Bailey, aged 13 years, bound to D.K. Justice until he attains the age of 21 years. E.M. Moore, security.

1874 Wednesday 4th August
   Page 139 James Lane appointed guardian of Fannie and George
   Chapman, minor children of William Chapman, decd. B.D. Harrold,
   security.

1875 Monday 6th September
   Page 150 W.C. Allen appointed guardian of Franklin and James Little,
   minors. Samuel W. Allen, security.

   Page 151 James Lane appointed guardian of Jane and James Chapman,
   children of William Chapman, decd. E.E. Bebber, security.

1875 Monday 4th October
   Page 175 J.L. Barker appointed guardian of Susan A., Margarett V.,
   Mary E., William L. and James H. Barker, minor children of the said
   J.L. Barker. Patrick Marshall and W.H. Kidwell, securities.

1874 Monday 1st November
   Page 187 Sparling Bowman appointed guardian of Kennedy and Mary
   Bowman, minor children of William and Amy Bowman, decd. Nelson
   S. Broyles, security.

1875 Monday 6th December
   Page 207 William Looney appointed guardian of George W. Crum, a
   minor child of Rachel and Andrew Crum, decd. William L. White,
   security.

1876 Monday 3rd January
   Page 238 A.E. Brummit appointed guardian of Margaret Brummit, a
   minor. Hulden Tucker, security.

   Jacob Mathews appointed guardian of John, Harriet and Thomas
   Mathews, minors. James Wright and Val S. Murry, securities.

1876 Monday 7th February
   Page 264 J.K.P. Keller appointed guardian of Sarah A. Keller,
   formerly Sarah A. Crumly, a minor. William Malone, security.

1876 Monday 6th March
   Page 280 William Dickson appointed guardian of James L., Mariah
   L., George W. and David H. Dickson, minor children of the said
   William Dickson. W.A. Allen, security.

   Page 281 Peter Harmon appointed guardian of Caroline, Mary and
   William Mayberry, minors. William A. Harmon, security.

   Page 282 R.C. Carter appointed guardian of J.L. Carter, a minor.
   John Hardin, security.

   Page 283 J.F. Davis appointed guardian of George F. and Sarah Jane
   Campbell, minors. Wiley Campbell, security.

1876 Monday 1st May
   Page 335 Mary Ann Burman? appointed guardian of Rachel Jane, Rutha
   A. and Frances G. Burman?, minor children of John S. Burman?, decd.
   John Kilday, security.

1876 Monday 5th June
   Page 350 Michael C. Meyers appointed guardian of Sarah Margaret
   Wells, a minor. W.H. Meyers, security.

   Page 351 R.M. Wright appointed guardian of Rebecca Jane Wright, a
   minor. Nathan Carter, security.

   Page 352 Nathan Carter appointed guardian of Mary Carter, a minor.
   R.M. Wright, security.

1876 Monday 3rd July
   Page 367 John Dearstone appointed guardian of Joseph L.V. Weems,
   a minor. Loyd R. Bullen and James H. Rose, securities.

1876 Monday 7th August
   Page 384 Jonathan W. Waddle appointed guardian of Sarah E. Waddle,

a minor. James Jones, security.

1876 Tuesday 8th August
Page 389 H.A. Bacon appointed guardian of Thomas, Charles and Jacob Bacon, minors. Sarah Bacon, security.

1876 Monday 4th September
Page 424 Mollie DeBusk appointed guardian of Clarissa Loretta Loppins, a minor. John Hinkle, security.

Thomas Morrow appointed guardian of Emaline Alexander, a minor. A.J. Alexander, security.

Page 426 M.V. Brazzledon appointed guardian of Martha Brazzledon, a minor. John P. Snapp, security.

1876 Monday 2nd October
Page 440 Rachel E. Smith appointed guardian of Mary Coggins, a minor child of Joshua Coggins, decd. William Smith, security.

Page 441 T.H. Brumly appointed guardian of David Alexander, Mary Louisa, John Crawford, Minervi Evaline and Andrew Theopholes Brumly, minors. W.L. Brumly, security.

1876 Tuesday 3rd October
Page 451 William C. Maloney appointed guardian of James, Martin L., Horace M., Samuel and Lulu Ayers, minors. John F. Hart and R.M. Maloney, securities.

1877 Monday 5th February
Page 500 D.A. Forester appointed guardian of Martha Jane, Cynthia, Elizabeth, Mary Ann, Thomas, Jesse Rosencrant and Sahra Ellen Hendry, minors. Abraham Lane, security.

Page 501 Abram Keller appointed guardian of James A. and John A. Weems, minors. E.K. Weems, security.

Page 502 T.R. McCollum appointed guardian of William, Ida, Sabina, Earley, Arthur and Virginia Smith, minors. William H. Meyers, security.

Elbert A. Brown appointed guardian of Mary M. Ellis, now Mary M. Brown, a minor. James H. Brown, security.

1877 Monday 5th March
Page 507 A.M. Smith appointed guardian of James Franklin Rogers and Margaret Rogers, minors. A.S. Johns and James K.R. Hall, sec.

Page 511 A.M. Bowman appointed guardian of Sparling J. Bowman and David A. Bowman, minor children of A.M. Bowman. William Looney, security.

Page 512 D.R. Gass appointed guardian of C.J. Russell, a minor. Thomas Russell, security.

1877 Monday 2nd April
Page 534 R.B. Weems appointed guardian of Ulyses G., R.B. and Rebecca Moore, minors. Abner J. Frazier, security.

Page 536 James Williams appointed guardian of Asburrey Brooks Williams, a minor. John B. Justice, security

Mary E. Honycut appointed guardian of Jacob D. Aston, a minor child of James Alexander Aston. Mary J. Ellison and William Rollins, securities.

Page 537 L.C. Akers appointed guardian of Wisley and Virginia Akers, minors. J.D. McMillan, security.

Enoch Hartman appointed guardian of Danil B., Joseph A., Emily V., and William C. Reed, minors. C.V. Hartman, security.

1877 Tuesday 3rd April
Page 547 Eliza Anderson appointed guardian of Sarah Margaret Anderson, a minor. John P. Carter and J.G. Weems, securities.

1877 Tuesday 3rd April
>Page 547 Eliza Anderson appointed guardian of Sarah Margaret
>Anderson, a minor. John P. Carter and J.G. Weems, securities.

1877 Monday 7th May
>Page 8 Jacob H. Broyles appointed guardian of David A. Broyles, a
>minor. James A. Broyles, security.

1877 Monday 4th June
>Page 23 Ruth Malinda Reynolds, aged 9 years on the 27th day of
>December last past, bound to Lucretia Tucker until she attains
>the age of 18 years. Joseph Hartman, security.
>
>Page 24 Robert C. Tipton, aged 6 years on the 28th day of August
>next, bound to John L. Helton until he attains the age of 21 years.
>J.M. Burgner, security.
>
>Elbert W. Tipton, aged 4 years on the 12th day of May last past,
>bound to John L. Heilton until he attains the age of 21 years.
>J.M. Burgner, security.
>
>John Murrel, aged 8 years on the 1st day of January last past,
>bound to A.H. Pierce until he attains the age of 21 years.
>J.K.P. Hall, security.

1877 Monday 2nd July
>Page 33 D.R. Gass appointed guardian of C.J. Russell, a minor.
>William A. Kidwell, security.
>
>Page 35 Oliver Holt appointed guardian of Stephen K. Hale, a minor.
>Henry Brown and Andrew Renner, securities.
>
>J.A. Baily appointed guardian of George W. Owens, a minor child of
>Benjamin F. Owens and Sarah E. Owens, decd. A.H. Jones, security.

1877 Monday 6th August
>Page 57 George Gass, Esqr. appointed guardian of Charles G. and
>Morgan A. Johnson, minors. William P. Hankins, security.
>
>George W. Laughlin appointed guardian of Julia A. and Andrew J.
>Laughlin, minors. G.B. Moncier, security.
>
>Page 58 W.G. Waddle appointed guardian of Delila C. and Mary E.
>Ricker, minors. W.J. Ruble, security.

1877 Monday 3rd September
>Page 76 G.S. Sentell appointed guardian of Kennedy Bowman and Mary
>Bowman, minors. William S. McGaughey, security.
>
>James A. Bible appointed guardian of Eliza C. Day, a minor. A.B.
>Ricker, security.
>
>D.W. Mercer appointed guardian of Nannie, James and Elizabeth
>Anderson, minors. Marshall Hartman, security.

1877 Tuesday 4th September
>Page 87 Sarah S. Gass, formerly Dunwoody, a minor over 14 years of
>age, chose John M. Gass as her guardian.

1877 Monday 1st October
>Page 104 Samuel H. Crawford appointed guardian of Thomas and
>Patience Gibson, minor children of Thomas Gibson, decd. A.N.
>Shaun, security.

1877 Monday 5th November
>Page 126 John Mysinger appointed guardian of William Mysinger, a
>minor. D.W. Mercer, security.

1877 Monday 3rd December
>Page 142 A.W. Walker appointed guardian of Jacob D. Aston, a minor
>child, under 16 years of age, of James M. Aston, decd. L.W.
>McInturf, security.
>
>Rufus Vance appointed guardian of Josephine, Jack and George
>Washington Broyles, minor children of Jackson Broyles, decd., late

a soldier of Co. H 1st Regt. U.S. Colard Artillery, War of 1861, and his wife Mary Broyle, now Jackson, by intermarriage with John Jackson. George E. Jones, security.

Sarenea C. Malicote appointed guardian of Mary F., William C., Charles A.H. and Lewis F. Malicote, minors. William H. Hunter, security.

1878 Monday 7th January
Page 152 Alexander Jane appointed guardian of Smith Henly, a minor child of Margaret Henley, decd. R.K. Waddle and S.S. Willhoit, securities.

Page 153 Houston Monroe, aged 3 years on the 13th day of October 1877, bound to John R. Low until he attains the age of 21 years. J.G. Gass, security.

1878 Monday 4th February
Page 176 Joseph Winters, aged 5 years on the 19th day of March last past, bound to A.C. Gregory until he attains the age of 21 years. William G. Ross, security.

T.J. Humphreys appointed guardian of Sarah Jane, Mary Alice, James Lyle and Alexander Humphreys, minors. John Peters and William H. Huffman, securities.

Page 177 Sarah Reeder appointed guardian of Elbert C. and Harvey E. Rader. Lemuel Crosby, security.

1878 Tuesday 5th February
Page 184 Lee Rutlege appointed guardian of Tennessee, George, William and Sallie Watterson, minors. William McGee, security.

1878 Monday 4th March
Page 193 M.L. Baily appointed guardian of James W. Baily, a minor. Hulden Tucker, security.

1878 Monday 1st April
Page 206 Mary A. Click appointed guardian of Andrew J. Pierce, minor child of Stephen A. Pierce, decd. John M. Click, security.

Cornelius Mays appointed guardian of Benjamin M. and Thomas C. Smith, minor children of Joseph Smith, decd. A.M. Smith, sec.

1878 Monday 6th May
Page 228 John Dearstone appointed guardian of Nancy E. Dearstone, a minor. M.G. Hybarger, security.

Page 231 William C. Woods, aged 3 years on the 17th day of July last past, bound to John F. Cooper until he attains the age of 21 years. Almegro Noele, security.

1878 Monday 1st July
Page 257 Stephen A. Ailshi appointed guardian of Lewis Andrew Ailshi, a minor. H.C. Smith, security.

James Tame appointed guardian of Wallace McAmis, a minor. Philip Babb, security.

John W. Wampler appointed guardian of Martha Emaline Wampler, a minor. William H. Myers, security.

C.M. Basket appointed guardian of Nancy Ann Rose and Mary Eliza Rose, minors. James H. Rose, security.

Page 262 H.L. McMillan appointed guardian of James, Samuel, Luther, Maynard, Catharine and Julia Ayers, minors. A.B. Hicks and Jeremiah McMillan, security.

1878 Monday 2nd September
Page 325 Samuel Malone, aged 5 years on the 25th day of November last past, bound to W.D. Weems until he attains the age of 21 years. J.D. Brown and J.R. Weems, securities.

Mary A. Brininstool? appointed guardian of Marcella Isabella and Matilda B. Hunt, minors. Archibald Babb, security.

1878 Monday 7th October
Page 346 Martha Farmer appointed guardian of Mary Emaline and Sarah C. Lones, minors. James Wampler and A.W. Cooter, securities.

Page 348 William W. Easterly appointed guardian of B.F., T.W., J.F. and R.E. Easterly, minors. M. Hale, security.

1878 Monday 4th November
Page 367 James H. Brown appointed guardian of Lydia I. and Mary E. Crumley, minors. William S. McCollum, security.

1878 Monday 2nd December
Page 384 Frederick Smelcer, aged 9 years on the 1st day of March last past, bound to James Evans until he attains the age of 21 years. W.A. Harmon, security.

1878 Tuesday 3rd December
Page 393 Mary Emaline Whitehead and James M. Whitehead, minors above the age of 14 years, chose M.F. Geralds as their guardian. John H. Brandon, security.

1879 Monday 3rd February
Page 425 L.W. Tipton appointed guardian of Lewis Tipton and George Tipton, two of his own minor children. A.W. Walker, security.

John A. Ottinger appointed guardian of Calvin, Wade and Emaline Hawk, minor heirs of Andrew Hawk, decd. John Hawk, security.

Henry A. Johnson appointed guardian of Henry, William P., Calvin, Francis, Mary Elizabeth, Nancy Anna, Nannie and Olnie Brooks, minor children of William Brooks, decd. William Johnson, security.

Page 426 Andrew Renner, Esqr. appointed guardian of James A., Mary E. and Alphie J. Walters, minors. Andrew Rader, security.

Joseph R. Smelcer, aged 13 years on the 7th day of February next, bound to J.E. Gosnell until he attains the age of 21 years. Enoch Hartman, security.

1879 Monday 7th April
Page 478 Edward Elenbaugh, aged 7 years, bound to W.A. Ottinger until he attains the age of 21 years. Abraham Rader, security.

1879 Tuesday 8th April
Page 488 William C. Smith appointed guardian of William Nelson and Martin Cornelius Smith, minors. Martin V. Bowman and A.M. Smith, securities.

1879 Thursday 13th May
Page 523 William Dodd appointed guardian of J.F., William G., Margaret, Martha, Sarah Jane, Mary M., M.F. and Richard Willet, minor children of Phillip Willet, decd. J.C. Jones and John W. Barun, securities.

1879 Monday 2nd June
Page 528 Olner D. Weems appointed guardian of Eliza Weems, a minor. G.F. Weems and Isaac B. Gray, securities.

1879 Monday 7th July
Page 547 Adam Knipp appointed guardian of Catharine, Julia Dinnah and Philip S. Cobble, minors. Christian Bible and Thomas Bible, securities.

Thomas Bible appointed guardian of Mary Ellen Cobble, a minor. Christian Bible and Adam Knipp, securities.

1879 Monday 1st September
Page 577 William A. Kidwell appointed guardian of Fannie G., Alice B. and Zulia Z. Kidwell, minors. Elijah Kidwell and W.P. Hankins, securities.

Page 579 Samuel E. Crawford appointed guardian of George A. and
Isaac B. Crawford, minors. Israel Smith and James B. Rodgers,
securities.

1879 Monday 6th October
Page 602 Mary J. Susong appointed guardian of Susan Susong, a child
of Andrew Susong, decd. A.E. Susong, security.

G.W. McCoy appointed guardian of Mary Elizabeth McCoy, a minor.
Daniel McCoy, security.

1879 Tuesday 4th November
Page 638 Will C. Brown appointed guardian of Jessee W. Brown, a
minor. Thomas S. Dobson and James T. Brown, securities.

1879 Monday 1st December
Page 8 C.W. Carr appointed guardian of Daniel K. Pierce and Martha
C. Pierce, minors. E.M. Moore and A.J. Mitchell, securities.

Page 9 James W. Waddle, aged 1 year on the 12th day of December
last past, bound to Martin Waddle until he attains the age of 21
years. W.R. Gibbs, security.

Page 10 Thomas M. Farmer appointed guardian of Caladona Winters, a
minor. A.S. Freshair, W.J. Ruble and James O. Fowler, securities.

Sidney Waddle, aged 2 years on the 30th day of December last past,
bound to Martin Waddle until he attains the age of 21 years. W.R.
Gibbs, security.

1880 Monday 5th January
Page 25 Alexander Pierce appointed guardian of Rebecca Jane Pierce,
a minor. Andrew English and Henry Monteith, securities.

John R. Weems appointed guardian of James C. Henry, a minor. Mary
Weems, security.

1880 Monday 2nd February
Page 55 Francis E. Hensley appointed guardian of Mary Ann, Fidilla,
James A., Francis E. and William B. Hensley. Charles L. Broyles,
security.

1880 Monday 1st March
Page 77 John M. Malone appointed guardian of Mary Ann Malone, a
minor. James D. Brown and J.M. Rhea, securities.

Page 79 David B. Hogan appointed guardian of James and David Evans,
minor children of Thomas A. Evans, decd. William Shields and James
T. Shields, securities.

Harriet L. Dickson appointed guardian of James C., Mary and Arte J.
Dickson, minors. William Russell and Stringfield Gass, securities.

1880 Monday 5th April
Page 97 W.C. Willis appointed guardian of James C., William
Jefferson, John Quinoy and Thela Cordelia Whitson, minor children
of William Winson, decd.

1880 Monday 2nd August
Page 185 J.C. Bunt appointed guardian of Caroline, P.S. and Julia
Cobble, minors. Christian Bible, N. Cobble and David Cobble,
securities.

Charles Brooks appointed guardian of Joseph N., Martha C., Susan
E., Francis E., Lorene? A. and Sofa Brooks, minors. S.K. Brooks
and C.A. Lovett, securities.

Page 186 W.H. Mynes appointed guardian of James Rader, a minor.
Madison Rader, M.C. Mynes, John M. Sup and Jacob M. Mynes, sec.

1880 Monday 4th October
Page 245 Samuel Pack appointed guardian of Barbara Ann Pack, a
minor. John Jordan and Elijah Pruitt, securities.

Nannie Anderson appointed guardian of Elizabeth and James Anderson, minors. John R. Armitage and Marshall Hartman, securities.

Page 247 I.P. Easterly appointed guardian of Joseph and Frederick Smelcer, minors. W.W. Easterly, William Smelcer, Franklin Hutson and Anderson Tappins, securities.

1880 Monday 1st November
Page 263 F.A. Hartman appointed guardian of Joseph and William Beck, minors. Christian Bible and Marshall Hartman, securities.

1880 Monday 5th December
Page 279 William B. McCord appointed guardian of John B., William C., Lewis A. and Lillie M. McCord, minors. John W. Willis, sec.

1881 Monday 3rd January
Page 293 C.J. Rader appointed guardian of James C. Erwin, a minor. A. Rader and James W. Bradford, securities.

1881 Monday 7th February
Page 308 M.M. Painter appointed guardian of Florance E., George L., McBiney and Horace H. Painter, minors. Area Painter and S.S. Wilhoit, securities.

Page 310 G.W. Gass appointed guardian of Mandy G. Hankins, a minor. John Gass and D.N. Ross, securities.

Charles F. Brooks appointed guardian of Michael F., Sarah L. and Ema L. Brooks, minors. S.H. Brooks and W.R. Gibbs, securities.

1881 Monday 7th March
Page 323 Wilson B. Johnson appointed guardian of George Alexander and Elizabeth Ann Johnson, minors. Daniel Kennedy and James Luster, securities.

1881 Monday 4th April
Page 334 James Keebler appointed guardian of James, Benjamin and Esther Smith, minor children of A.M. Smith, decd. Fethias Woolsey and C. Mays, securities.

1881 Monday 6th June
Page 386 Samuel K. McGaughy appointed guardian of George M. and Edie S. McGaughy, minors. W.S. McGaughy and R.A. McGaughy, sec.

1881 Tuesday 5th July
Page 401 J.B. Fraker appointed guardian of Florance C. Fraker, a minor. J.M. Fraker and G.H. Mahony, securities.

Samuel B. Winslow appointed guardian of John and Albert Triper, minors. Clay Shaun, security.

Page 402 W.H. Triper appointed guardian of Fannie Triper, a minor. W.I. Dodd and J.B.R. Lyon, securities.

1881 Monday 1st August
Page 439 J.A. Small appointed guardian of Joseph B. and Anna B. Small, his own minor children. W.I. Dodd and C.S. Rankin, sec.

1881 Monday 5th September
Page 458 Adam M. Jane appointed guardian of Addri and Mary Jane, minor children of Thomas W. Jane, decd. Alexander Jane and C.H. Bird, securities.

1881 Monday 3rd October
Page 477 George Click appointed guardian of Andrew J. Pierce, minor child of Stephen Pierce, decd. S.S. Wilhoit, security.

1881 Monday 7th November
Page 498 Robert M. Stephens appointed guardian of L.V.M. Stephens, a minor. S.J. Stephens and Fox Stephens, securities.

Persons Names	Quantity of Land in Each Tract	Situation or Place Where Each Tract Lies	Material Circumstances of the Title	Common School Lands	No. of White Polls	No. of Town Lots	No. of Slaves	No. of Stud Horses	Pleasure Carriages
ALLEN, Joseph	400	Sink Creek					3		
ALLEN, James	155	Sink Creek			1				
ARMSTRONG, John	363½	Sink Creek			1				
ALLISON, William					1				
ALLISON, John	230	Limestone		110	1				
ARMSTRONG, Alex.					1				
BAYLES, Solomon	208½								
BAYLES, Samuel					1				
BAYLES, Jacob	375				1				
BAYLES, Mary				160					
BARACROFT, Jno.	375								
BAYLES, Stephen					1				
BERDWELL, James					1				
BERDWELL, John					1				
CRABTREE, William	50				1				
CARSON, Thomas	118	Limestone			1		7		
CREMER, Thomas	193				1				
CILLY, Peggy	68								
COLLINS, Uriah				12½					
COLLET, Abraham	449				1				
COLLET, Isaac					1				
COLLET, John					1				
COCKBURN, James					1				
DOTSON, Edmund	272	Celar B.							
DOTSON, Peter					1				
DOTSON, Reuben					1				
DOTSON, James					1				
DOTSON, Charles					1				
DINWIDDIE, James	386½	Mill fork					1		
DINWIDDIE, Jas. H.					1				
DINWIDDIE, Wm. R.	80	Mill fork			1				
DINWIDDIE, John	30				1				
DENWIDDIE, John	54				1				
DUNCAN, Samuel	117	Millfork			1		1		
FRAKER, John	86				1				
FRAKER, Frederick	153				1				
FRAKER, Adam	400								
FRAKER, John Jr.	325			125					
FRAKER, Michael	100				1				
FALLS, James	50				1				
FALLS, John				5					
GILLESPIE, Geo. H.	327	Limestone		50	1		3		
Same Guardian for Wm. McMACKE	65								
GILLESPIE, Allen	900						16		
HACKEN, Isaac C.				186	1				
HENRY, Robert	208¾	Millfork					1		
HOUSTON, John	86	Millfork	Entry	15	1				
HUNT, Thomas	130	Millfork			1				
HAYS, Samuel	90				1				
HOPE, Menor					1				
HARIS, John					1				
HARTMAN, Levi	193				1				

Persons Names	Quantity of Land in Each Tract	Situation or Place Where Each Tract Lies	Material Circumstances of the Title	Common School Lands	No. of White Polls	No. of Town Lots	No. of Slaves	No. of Stud Horses	Pleasure Carriages
JUSTIS, John	125	Millfork			1				
JONES, John					1				
KILE, Henry					1				
KENNEDY, William	234								
KENNEDY, Joseph	270				1	1			
KENNEDY, George					1				
LOYD, John	120	Sinking C.			1				
LOYD, Roberson					1				
LOYD, Abel					1				
LOYD, Thos. Senr.	160	Limestone							
MILLER, John	162	Millfork			1	1			
McMACKEN, John	112				1				
MILBURN, Wm. Jr.	100				1				
MILBURN, Wm. Sr.	56		Entry	24					
McMACKIN, James	121				1				
MILBURN, Joseph	126				1				
MILBURN, Wm. Jr. Guardian for Jonathan	44								
MYERS, John	248	Millfork							
MYERS, James					1				
MERCER, Elbert					1				
MERCER, Absalom					1				
MORGAN, Stephen					1				
McNEESE, Gravener					1				
McNEESE, Samuel	608½								
NAFF, Abraham	65		Entry	50	1		1		
NAFF, Jonathan	181						1		
PAYNE, John					1				
PRAT, Kiles					1				
PAYNE, Patsy	75	Cedar Br.							
ROSS, Edward	177			23					
ROBERTS, Thomas					1				
ROBERTS, John					1				
RUSTIN, Robert					1				
SELLERS, Sol. W.					1				
STANBURY, Jacob					1				
STANBURY, Ezekiel					1				
SEXTON, Absalom					1				
SEXTON, Allen					1				
SHANKS, Silas	50				1				
SHANKS, David R.					1				
SHANKS, Holden					1				
SHANKS, Moses					1				
SHANKS, Silas Exc.	129								
SHANKS, William					1				
TELLER, David					1				
TEDLOCK, Sevier	186				1				
Same	519½	Sink C.			1		1		
WALICE, John	251				1		1		
WILLIAMS, Wm.					1				

Persons Names	Quantity of Land in Each Tract	Situation or Place Where Each Tract Lies	Material Circumstances of the Title	Common School Lands	No. of White Polls	No. of Town Lots	No. of Slaves	No. of Stud Horses	Pleasure Carriages
BRIGHT, Michael Sr	500	Sinking Br. of Lick Crk.							
The same joining these Entries	99		3 deed Grants						
The same ELLIS place	240		deed						
The same Entries	62		deed						
The same two Entries bought of Daniel ROBISON	80		deed						
The same DITTAMORE place	250	Sinking Ck.	deed						
The same for Entries joining	10		Grant						
The same bought of Thomas COLLIER	168	Clear fork	Deed						
BRIGHT, David					1				
BRIGHT, Michael Jr	277	do	Deed		1				
The same for	26								
BASKET, William	200	Lick Creek	Deed	40	1				
BRANDON, Thos. Sr.	187	do	do	62½		1			
BRANDON, James	25	do	do		1				
BRANDON, William	233				1				
BRANDON, John	38				1				
BRANDON, Thos. Jr.					1				
BAXTER, Hail					1	1			
BAXTER, James					1				
BRIT, Mary Wid.	20	do	deed	20	1	1			
BINHAM, John				50	1				
BAXTER, Barnett	87	Clearfork	deed	9	1				
BAXTER, Edmund	144	do	do	20½	1				
COULSTON, Thomas	230	do	do						
COULSTON, Elijah	105	Longfork	do						
CRAWFORD, John	166	Lick Creek	do	42		1			
The same as guardian for William	100	do							
The same for	150	do	do						
CAMPBELL, James					1				
CALDWELL, Samuel	350		do	13	1				
CALDWELL, Alex.					1				
CALDWELL, James					1				
COLLIER, Rebeka	253	Clearfork							
CORDER, Jonathan					1				
CORDER, John					1				
CRAWFORD, Samuel					1				
COLE, Philip	7								
CALDWELL, Thomas	119	Clearfork	deed						
The same for	30			30					
The same for	15		Grant						
The same for	12		do						
DOBBINS, Andrew	200	Lick Creek	Deed						
DOBBINS, William					1				
DEATHERAGE, John					1				
DELANEY, Benjamin	114¾	Lick Creek	Deed						

Persons Names	Quantity of Land in Each Tract	Situation or Place Where Each Tract Lies	Material Circumstances of the Title	Common School Lands	No. of White Polls	No. of Town Lots	No. of Slaves	No. of Stud Horses	Pleasure Carriages
ENGLISH,									
John Mountain	100	do	do	3	1				
ENGLISH, Alex,	319	Clearfork	deed	34			3	$1	
The same	40	do							
The same for	60	do							
The same	300	do	deed						
The same	137	do	do						
ENGLISH, John of									
Alexander					1				
ENGLISH, Andrew					1				
ENGLISH, Thomas	132	Lick Creek	deed	146	1				
ENGLISH, John	100	Horse Creek							
FINCHER, John	32	Clearfork	deed	128					
FINCHER, Joseph					1				
FINCHER, Richard					1				
GENTRY, Simons	100	Longfork	deed						
GENTRY, Richard					1				
GRAY, Robert Sr.	916	do	do				1		
GRAY, Robert Jr.	150				1				
GILLIS, John					1				
HALL, William	621	Lick Creek	Deed	42			2		
HALL, Dimon					1				
HAYS, Charles					1				
HARROLD, Amasa	92	Clearfork	do	22					
HARROLD, Andrew M.					1				
HAIL, Mashack	150	do	do	27			3		
HALL, James	67½	Horse Creek	do	156	1				
HAIL, Lewis				120					
HAIL, Mashach Jr.				39	1				
HALL, Joseph for									
the heirs of				11					
Samuel HALL decd.									
HACKER, Jacob Sr.	50	Clear Creek	deed						
HACKER, Jacob Jr.					1				
HACKER, James					1				
HAYS, Joseph Sr.	108	Longfork	Deed		1				
The same for	70	do	do						
The same for	75								
The same for the									
old place	121								
HARROLD, Jesse	64	L. Creek	do		1				
HAYS, William	130	L. Creek	do	30		1			
HAYS, George	218	Clearfork	do		1				
HAYS, Robert	239	Longfork	do				1		
The same for the									
old place	78¼	do	do						
HAYS, John of Robt					1				
HAYS, John of Dav.					1				
HAYS, Joseph L.	45	Longfork	Deed		1				
HALL, David					1				
HAYS, Isaac					1				
HAYS, Aaron					1				
JOHNSTON, John	60	Clearfork	Deed		1				
JACKSON, William	300	Lick Creek	do		1				

Persons Names	Quantity of Land in Each Tract	Situation or Place Where Each Tract Lies	Material Circumstances of the Title	Common School Lands	No. of White Polls	No. of Town Lots	No. of Slaves	No. of Stud Horses	Pleasure Carriages
JOHNSTON, Jas. Sr.	289	Clearfork	Deed						
The same for	21	do		60					
JOHNSTON, Jas. Jr.					1				
JOHNSTON, William					1				
MOORE, Abraham	112	Horse Creek	do						
Same	47	Joining Saml. EDGMON							
MONTEETH, George	90	Long fork	do	79	1				
The same	119	do	do						
MULLINEX,									
Elizabeth, Widow	27	Lick Creek	do	28					
MORELOCK, Nathan					1				
McFERSON, Daniel					1				
MONTEETH, Henry Jr					1				
McDANIEL, John	119	Clearfork	Deed	20	1				
The same for	121	do	do						
The same	8	do	do						
MOORE, Abraham Jr.	16¾	Horse Creek	do	4	1				
MOORE, William	10	do	do	50	1				
NEEL, Stodart	200	Clearfork	do	19	1				
PEARCE, Jonathan					1				
POPE, Simon	91	Lick Creek	Deed	30			2		
PICKERING, Nancy	213	Sinking Crk.	do						
PICKERING, Ellis	165	Cedar Br.			1				
PHILIPS, Charles	189	Clearfork			1				
PICKINS, Robt. K.	225			16			2		
PEARCE, Richard				25	1				
RHEA, John Esqr.	426	Lick Creek	do	30		2			
ROBISON, George	69	Clearfork	do		1				
ROBSON, John	95	do		89	1				
RODGERS, John M.	421	Lick Creek	deed	120	1		3	$150	
RODGERS, James					1				
RHEA, Charles					1				
RYAN, Robert	357	Clearfork	do		1		1		
RECTOR, Benjamin	201	Clearfork	Deed						
The same for	150			22					
REGISTER, Francis	240	L. Creek	Deed						
ROBINSON, Jacob	100	Horse Creek	Deed						
ROW, William					1				
ROBISON, Joseph					1				
SHANKS, Moses	193	Lick Creek	Deed	200	1				
SMITH, Turner	212	do	do		1				
SMITH, Hiram	50	do	do	50	1				
STONECYPHER, Henry					1				
SLATEN, Kiah					1				
SHANKS, James	50	do	do	258	1				
SHACKLEFORD, Dav.					1				
SHEALS, William	144	do			1				
TADLOCK, James	200	Clearfork	Deed		1				
WHEELER, Isaac	206	Lick Creek							
WHEELER, James					1				
WHITE, Richard	115	Clearfork	Deed	115	1				
WOOLSEY, Frethias	175	Lick Creek	do	125	1				

Persons Names	Quantity of Land in Each Tract	Situation or Place Where Each Tract Lies	Material Circumstances of the Title	Common School Lands	No. of White Polls	No. of Town Lots	No. of Slaves	No. of Stud Horses	Pleasure Carriages
WILLIAMS, Hugh	100	do	do	60					
WEST, James					1				
Taken by Samuel CALDWELL									

CAPTAIN JOHNSON'S COMPANY

Persons Names	Quantity of Land in Each Tract	Situation or Place Where Each Tract Lies	Material Circumstances of the Title	Common School Lands	No. of White Polls	No. of Town Lots	No. of Slaves	No. of Stud Horses	Pleasure Carriages
BARKLEY, William	394	Sinking	Deed		1				
BRITTON, James					1				
BABB, Joshua	⅓	do	do		1				
BAILES, Jacob	160½	do	do		1				
BAILES, Solomon	135¾	do	do						
BROWN, Hannah	84	do	Bond						
BROWN, W.					1				
BROWN, Thomas	208	Mire Bran.	deed						
BROWN, Isaac					1				
BAILES, Elihu	56	Mc. Bran.	do		1				
COLLANS, Charles	½				1				
CRUMLEY, Abraham					1				
DEPEW, James	219	Cedar Br.	do		1				
DILLON, Laban					1				
DILLON, William	257	Sinking	Will		1				
DILLON, Peter	142	Mets	ditto		1				
DILLON, James	288	Sinking	ditto						
DILLON, Garrett	241	do	deed						
DELANEY, Daniel	108	do	do		1				
ditto guardian for David DELANEY	100	do	do						
EARNEST, John					1				
EARNEST, Joseph					1				
ELLIS, Jacob	160½	do	do		1				
ELLIS, Jonathan	130¾	do	do		1				
ELLIS, Jesse	106	do	do		1				
ELLIS, Jonathan					1				
ELLIS, Jesse	30	Mire Br.	do		1				
FRIEZE, David	130	McCarters	Will		1				
FRIEZE, Jacob	192½	Chucky	deed		1				
FRIEZE, John	100	Mc. Bran.	Will		1				
FRAZIER, Abner Jr.	831½	Sinking	deed						
FRAZIER, Abner	100	Rogers B.	Will		1				
GRAY, John	12	McCarters	Deed		1				
GAUNTT, Samuel	468	Big Sinking	do						
GAUNTT, Malachi					1				
GRAY, Benjamin	133	M. Branch	do		1				
GRUBS, Samuel					1				
GRUBS, John					1				
GAUNTT, Kelle	112	Sinking	do		1				
HENDERSON, George	178	McMount			1		1		

Persons Names	Quantity of Land in Each Tract	Situation or Place Where Each Tract Lies	Material Circumstances of the Title	Common School Lands	No. of White Polls	No. of Town Lots	No. of Slaves	No. of Stud Horses	Pleasure Carriages
HOPE, Baty N.	93				2				
HARROLD, Jonathan	11¼	Sinking	do						
HARROLD, Uriah	4	do	do		1				
HORNBURGER, Jacob	344	do	do				2		
HUMBERT, Henry					1				
HENDERSON, Alex.	243	Sinking Ck.	do		1				
HENDERSON, Robt.Sr						1			
HENDERSON, Joseph	327¾	Sinking	do		1		2		
HENDERSON, Rob. Jr					1				
HARROLD, Elijah					1				
HAMMER, Aaron	84	McCart	do		1				
HUNLEY, John S.					1				
JOHNSON, William	139	Sinking	Deed		1				
JOHNSON, Thomas					1				
LINSFIELD, Sexton					1				
LIKENS, William	50	Mcty.	do		1				
LEWIS, Peter					1				
McCLURE, Robert	135¾	L. Sinking	do		1				
MOLSBURGER, Mica					1				
MORELOCK, George	329	Sinking	do				1		
MORELOCK, Jonathan					1				
MILBURN, Jonathan	149	do	do		1				
MARSHILL, John	59	McCarter	do		1				
McKEEHAN, George					1				
McNEESE, Saml. Jr.					1				
McNEESE, Samuel	608½	Sinking	do		1				
MARSH, Gravenor	206	do	do						
ditto	272	Store Br.							
MILLS, Ritch					1				
MATTHEWS, John					1				
PEARSE, Thomas					1				
PETERS, Samuel agent for	150	Sinking	do		1				
Fredk. WEAVER									
RIPLEY, Henry	56	Bullans run	Bond		1				
REESE, Jonathan					1				
REESE, Moses	400	Sinking	deed						
ROGERS, John	210	do	Will				1		
REESE, John	391¾	do	do		1				
REESE, William					1				
REESE, Solomon					1				
RIPLEY, Thomas	116	McCart.	deed		1				
RIPLEY, Samuel	316	McBranch	do		1				
RIPLEY, Phebe	95	Bullars	Dowry					1	
REESE, John					1			1	$1.50
SQUIBB, Caleb	126	McBranch	Deed		1				
SMALL, Daniel	125	Sinking	do						
SMALL, Benjamin					1				
SIMPSON, Robert					1				
SIMPSON, Elias	72½	do	Bond		1				
SIMPSON, John	332½	do	Deed						
STANFIELD, David	254½	Sinking	Deed		1			1	.75
STANFIELD, Samuel	145	do	do						

CAPTAIN JOHNSON'S COMPANY

Persons Names	Quantity of Land in Each Tract	Situation or Place Where Each Tract Lies	Material Circumstances of the Title	Common School Lands	No. of White Polls	No. of Town Lots	No. of Slaves	No. of Stud Horses	Pleasure Carriages
STANFIELD, Thomas	61	Mcternes	do		1				
TAYLOR, Allen					1				
TAYLOR, Britton					1				
THORNBURG, Elisha	41	Sinking	do		1				
THORNBURG, Morgan	56	do	do		1				
TAYLOR, James					1				
TUCKER, John	200	Lick C.	do						
THOMPSON, James					1				
WHINNERY, Joseph	80	Sinking	do		1				
WRIGHT, Jacob	55½	do	Will		1				
WRIGHT, John					1				
WRIGHT, Jesse	112½	Mire branch	deed						
WHITE, Daniel					1				
Taken by John MATTHEWS, Justice of Peace									

CAPTAIN KELLEY'S COMPANY

Persons Names	Quantity of Land in Each Tract	Situation or Place Where Each Tract Lies	Material Circumstances of the Title	Common School Lands	No. of White Polls	No. of Town Lots	No. of Slaves	No. of Stud Horses	Pleasure Carriages
ALEXANDER, Thomas	360			20			1		
ALEXANDER, Stph. K	106				1		4		
ALEXANDER, King W.					1				
ALEXANDER, Thomas of Stephen	124								
ALEXANDER, John	100				1				
ALEXANDER, Thomas of Thomas					1				
ALEXANDER, David					1				
ALEXANDER, King W. for Polly ALEXANDER							1		
BABB, Thomas	150								
BRITTON, Wm. of WM									
BULLIN, Joseph	150	Ho. Cr.			1		1		
BRATTON, J. C.					1				
BARRUM, Hawbart					1				
BRIDEWELL, Samuel	100				1				
CREMON, John	165	CR			1				
CRUMON, Daniel	550								
CRIGGEN, Thomas					1				
DOAK, Samuel W.	663			87	1		4		
DODD, William									
DODD, John									
DODD, Rudolph									
DOBSON, Silas	192	fC			1		1		
DUNWOODY, Adam	132				1				
ELLIS, Samuel	198				2				
FORTNER, Jonathan					1				
FORTNER, Wiley					1				

Persons Names	Quantity of Land in Each Tract	Situation or Place Where Each Tract Lies	Material Circumstances of the Title	Common School Lands	No. of White Polls	No. of Town Lots	No. of Slaves	No. of Stud Horses	Pleasure Carriages
GRAY, Asar	178			50	1				
GUINN, Polly	300								
HAWORTH, Ann	48								
HOWEL, Andrew					1				
HENRY, Ewen					1				
HOYAL, Jacob	63			12					
HOYAL, Philip	350				1			1 $1	
HOWEL, John					1				
HAWORTH, Silas	125				1				
HAWORTH, Mary	119								
HAWORTH, Nathaniel	220				1				
HAWORTH, West	140				1				
JOHNSON, Benjamin	197				1				
KENNEDY, John	382				1				
KELLY, James	131	H.C.			1				
LIKENS, Gravener					1				
LOW, Hugh					1				
LAUGHLIN, Alex.					1				
MOORE, John					1				
MURPHY, Thomas	150	H.C.		237			1		
MARSH, James	334				1				
McCORD, Thomas	106	H.C.		65	1				
McCORD, Esther	168	H.C.					1		
MILBURN, John					1				
MORROW, James	107								
MORROW, John	212								
MOORE, David	400			10	2				
MOORE, James	50				1				
McCAMISH, John	221	S.C.		35	3				
McCAMISH, Samuel	139	L.C.			1				
McCAMISH, George	102			25	1				
MARSHALL, Martha	234								
MARSHALL, Isaac	47				1				
MARSHALL, Joseph					1				
OLIPHANT, James	186	S.C.		26	1		2		
OLIPHANT, John	100	S.C.			1				
PETERS, Warner					1				
PAYNE, Merryman	168¾			4½	1	2	2		
RIPLEY, William	144½				1				
RANKEN, Robert	467	H.C.			1		4		
ROBINSON, John	100			3	1		1		
ROBERTS, Jesse	100	S.C.		30	1				
ROSS, James	398	H.C.			1		3		
ROSS, Wm. Junr.	186	R.F.			1		1		
REAH, Ezekiel	114				1				
RANKIN, David	1254¾						6		
RANKIN, Lewis	20								
ROBINSON, James	174				1		1		
REAH, Robert	31				1				
ROBINSON, Samuel	555						2		
ROBINSON, Jas. Jr.	194½				1				
REED, John S.				8			3		

CAPTAIN KELLEY'S COMPANY

Persons Names	Quantity of Land in Each Tract	Situation or Place Where Each Tract Lies	Material Circumstances of the Title	Common School Lands	No. of White Polls	No. of Town Lots	No. of Slaves	No. of Stud Horses	Pleasure Carriages
STANFIELD, William	135				1				
SMITH, George	220				1				
SHAW, James					1				
STONECYPHER, Jos.					1				
SIMPSON, Jas. C.					1				
STRAIN, John				60					
THOMPSON, Solomon					1				
THOMPSON, Thomas					1				
WILLIS, Sylvanus					1				
WILLIS, James					1				
WEST, Richard	46¾	H.C.			1	1	1		
WILSON, David	212				2				
WILLIAMS, Mary	250								

John S. REED
Justice of the Peace

CAPTAIN WILLIAM HUMBERD'S COMPANY 1830 (formerly HAYNE'S)

Persons Names	Quantity of Land in Each Tract	Situation or Place Where Each Tract Lies	Material Circumstances of the Title	Common School Lands	No. of White Polls	No. of Town Lots	No. of Slaves	No. of Stud Horses	Pleasure Carriages
BABB, Henry	30	H.C. fork	Title	50	1				
BOO, Rudolph	128½	do	do						
BAILEY, Martin	626¼	Sinking Ck.	do		1		2		
BAILEY, Jacob	198½	do	do						
Same for the heir of Isaac Bailes	7	do	do						
BRUNER, Daniel					1				
BRIGHT, Charles	401	H.C. fork	do		1				
BABB, Seth Junr.	88¾	Horse Fork	do		1				
BRUNER, Joseph	25	do		16	1				
BABB, Isaac	260	W.S. Creek	do		1		1		
Same	190	Head of S.C.	do						
CAMPBELL, Archi.	300	S.C.	do		1		1		
COTTER, James Sr.	436	Dunhams fk.	do	5	1				
COTTER, James Jr.					1				
COTTER, George					1				
CRADDICK, William				50	1				
CRABTREE, Barnett, heirs of	95	Sinking Ck.	do						
CRABTREE, John					1				
CRABTREE, Henry					1				
CRABTREE, Barnett					1				
DODD, William	196	W of Chucky	do	32					
DOTY, Azariah	200	H.C. fork	do	50			1		
DOTY, Ephraim	'				1				
DOTY, Jesse	5	do	do	4	1				
DODD, John Jr.	18ⁱ²	do	do	48	1				
DUNKIN, Joseph	183	do	do				2		
DAVIS, Nathaniel	100	Dunhams fd.	do	22	1				
Same	180	Tilman fork	do						
Same	100	W.S. Creek	do						

CAPTAIN WILLIAM HUMBERD'S COMPANY 1830 (formerly HAYNE'S)

Persons Names	Quantity of Land in Each Tract	Situation or Place Where Each Tract Lies	Material Circumstances of the Title	Common School Lands	No. of White Polls	No. of Town Lots	No. of Slaves	No. of Stud Horses	Pleasure Carriages
DICKSON, John	320	Sinking Br.	do				1		
DAVIS, James					1				
FORD, Mary	28	H.C. fork	do						
FANNON, Alfred					1				
GRUBS, William					1				
GRUBS, Edwin	140	Sinking Br.	do						
GRUBS, Ameris					1				
HUMBERD, Adin	127	H.C. fork	do	19½					
HUMBERD, William					1				
HUMBERD, Jno. Sr.	100	H.C. fork	do						
HUMBERD, Jno. Jr.					1				
HUMBERD, Samuel					1				
HUMBERD, John					1				
HOGGATT, Anthony	108	H.C. fork	do		1				
HOGGATT, Nathan									
HERRALD, Jonathan	57½	H.C. fork	do	20	1				
HERRALD, Amasa	147		do		1				
HAYNES, Azariah					1				
HAYNES, Abraham	100	Horse fork	do						
HOLLAND, Andrew					1				
HOLLAND, Abrm. Jr.				66	1				
JONES, James	468	H.C. fork	do	5					
Same for the heirs of Jesse DAVIS, decd.	160	W.L. Creek	do						
JOHNSTON, William	120	Roaring Fk.	do						
LANE, Samuel	35	H.C. fork	do	19					
LANE, William					1				
LOGAN, David	78	L.C.	do	138					
Same	65	Long fork	do						
MILLIKEN, Samuel	100	H.C. fork	do		1				
MALTSBARGER, Geo.	172	Middle Crk.	do		1				
MALTSBARGER, John John Sr.	613	W.S. Creek	do	25					
MALTSBARGER, John Jr.					1				
McCOLLUM, James	300	H.C. fork	do		1			1	1 $1 50
Same for the heirs of T. McCOLLUM, decd.	129½	L. Creek							
McCOLLUM, John	297	do	do	50	1	1			
McNEES, William		W.L. Creek		170	1				
McNEESE, Evin	100			11	1				
Same by Warrant	5								
MOORE, James Sr.	250	W.S. Creek	Title	175					
MAYS, Jesse				130	1				
MAYS, Peter				50	1				
MANNING, John				170	1				
MULLINS, William					1				
MILLER, Jacob					1				
McNEESE, Marmaduke					1				
NIXON, Robert					1				

CAPTAIN WILLIAM HUMBERD'S COMPANY 1830 (formerly HAYNE'S)

Persons Names	Quantity of Land in Each Tract	Situation or Place Where Each Tract Lies	Material Circumstances of the Title	Common School Lands	No. of White Polls	No. of Town Lots	No. of Slaves	No. of Stud Horses	Pleasure Carriages
NEWMAN, Jacob					1				
OLINGER, Sylvanus	330	Grassy Crk.	do		1				
OLINGER, John	250	S.C.	do	27	1				
PICKERING, Ellis	165	Cedar Br.	do						
PICKERING, Phinihas					1				
STONECYPHER, Abrm.	682¼	South fork	do						
STONECYPHER, Abraham Jr.					1				
STONECYPHER, Sol.	103¾	Horse fork	do						
SMITH, Cornelius Senr.	185	Long fork	do	50	1				
SMITH, Cornelius Junr.	180	do	do	100	1				
SMITH, John				125	1				
SMITH, Joseph					1				
SMITH, Aaron					1				
STONECYPHER, John					1				
THOMASON, William				87½	1				
THOMASON, Howel					1				
THOMPSON, Alex.					1				
THOMPSON, Thomas					1				
WHITE, Joseph	76	do							
WHITE, Jacob	100	H.C. fork	do	200					
WHITE, Henry					1				
WHITE, Robert					1				
WHITE, Bloomer	93	H.C. fork	do						
WOODS, William				100	1				
WALKER, Lee					1				
WALKER, Samuel					1				
WHITE, John, heirs of	107	Cedar Br.	Title						
WOOLSEY, Fethias	175	W.S. Creek	title	25	1				
WHITE, Abraham					1				
YEAKLEY, Henry, heirs of	134	do	do	20					
YEAKLEY, Isaiah				50	1				
YEAKLEY, George					1				
		By Charles BRIGHT J. P.							

CAPTAIN DELLS COMPANY 1830

AKERSON, George					1				
BABB, Philip Sr.	200	Tilmans fk.	Title	61					
BABB, Samuel					1				
BABB, Seth Senr.	120	do	do						
BRITTON, William	196	do							

Persons Names	Quantity of Land in Each Tract	Situation or Place Where Each Tract Lies	Material Circumstances of the Title	Common School Lands	No. of White Polls	No. of Town Lots	No. of Slaves	No. of Stud Horses	Pleasure Carriages
BRADLY, Joseph				70	1				
BABB, Abner	103	do		34	1				
BENNETT, James	40		do	50	1				
BOWMAN, Jacob Sr.	900	L. Ck.					7		
BROWN, William	150	L. C.		18	1				
BOWMAN, Joseph					1		1		
BOWMAN, Samuel	490	Lk	do	48	1				
BRUNER, Joseph	25	Horse fork	do	16	1				
BRIENT, John					1				
CARTER, Hugh	266	do	do	240	1		1		
DODD, Thomas	388½	do	do	378	1				
DELL, Henry	225	Lk	do		1		1		
DAVIS, Sarah	180								
DOTY, Azariah	200	Horse fork	do				1		
DOTY, Ephraim					1				
GASS, John Sr.	1150	Rorg. fork	do				8		
GASS, William	56½	D. fork	do	47½	1				
GASS, John M.	56	do	do	90	1				
HAWKINS, Saml. S.	60	D. fork	do	110	1				
HOUTS, Christopher	588	Lk	do	100					
HAWKINS, Nathan	80	L. fork	do	82	1				
Same	29	Horse fork							
HARVEY, Smith				120	1				
HENDRY, Gabriel					1				
HIBERGER, Samuel					1				
HENDRY, William	187½	L. Ck.	Title	200					
Same	220	S. Ck.	do						
HENDRY, Thornton	50	do	do	100	1				
JUSTIS, Isaac	66	D. fork	do	100					
JUSTIS, Thomas					1				
JUSTIS, John					1				
JONES, Alexander					1				
LINEBAUGH, Jn. Jr.	230	Lk	do						
LINEBAUGH, Jac. Sr	211	Lk		200			1		
LANE, John					1				
LANE, Dutton	100	Lk.	do	12	1				
LINEBAUGH, Jacob					1				
LINEBAUGH, Samuel	136	Lk.	do	140					
McCAMISH, William	160	Cedar Br.	do	100	1				
MELONE, Joseph	82	Dry fork	do	110	1				
MORRISON, Wesley	131	Lk.	do		1				
MORRISON, Elijah	117	Lk.	do		1				
MORRISON, William									
McCURRY, Joseph	120	T. fork	do	25	1		1		
McCURRY, John Sr.	220	do	do	50					
McCURRY, John Jr.	200	do	do		1				
MILIKAN, Samuel	100	do	do		1	Return in H			
MILIKAN, John					1				
RUSSELL, William					1				
STARNES, Leonard	264	do	do		1				
STARNES, Jacob					1				

CAPTAIN DELLS COMPANY 1830

Persons Names	Quantity of Land in Each Tract	Situation or Place Where Each Tract Lies	Material Circumstances of the Title	Common School Lands	No. of White Polls	No. of Town Lots	No. of Slaves	No. of Stud Horses	Pleasure Carriages
SIMPSON, James					1				
THOMPSON, Absalom	331	Lk.	do	40	1				
THOMPSON, John Sr.	50	D. fork	do	20					
WHITE, Abraham	100	T. fork	do	25					
WHITE, Frederick	50	Lk.	do	50	1				
WHITECERS, William					1				
WHICKERS, William					1				
Taken & Returned by Leonard STARNES Esqr.									

CAPTAIN HENRY TARRANTS COMPANY 1830

Persons Names	Quantity of Land in Each Tract	Situation or Place Where Each Tract Lies	Material Circumstances of the Title	Common School Lands	No. of White Polls	No. of Town Lots	No. of Slaves	No. of Stud Horses	Pleasure Carriages
BROWN, David	200	Churn C. Ck.	do	59¼					
BUNAR, Samuel					1				
BLANDON, John	93	Puncheon Ck.	do		1				
BALEY, Thos. Jr.	82½	Little Gap	do	142	1				
BALEY, Thos. Sr.	318½	ditto	do						
BROWN, James	100	Camp Creek	do		1				
BROWN, David of Thomas					1				
BRUNAR, Aughnal	51	Dry fork	do						
BRUNAR, Jacob	247	Ditto	do						
BABB, Philip	100	Churn Camp	do		1				
BROTHERTON, Wm.	150	Big Gap	do	150				1	1$1
BROWN, Silvan of David					1				
COUCH, John Jr.				140	1				
COOTAR, Philip	200	Plum Creek	do						
COOTAR, John	108	Camp Creek	do						
CARTER, Elisha	445	Plomp Creek	do	249	1				
CARTER, Ezekiel of Jn.	60	Puncheon Ck	do	100	1				
CARTER, Samuel	65	ditto	do	140	1				
CARTER, Nathan	200	ditto	do						
CARTER, Benjm. Jr.	150	ditto	do	177	1				
CARTER, John of Nat.				55	1				
CARTER, Elias	45	Punchin Ck.	do	140	1				
Same Adm. of Hiram CARTER dcd	30	do	do						
CHILDERS, Joseph					1				
CARTER, Abel					1				
COUCH, Peter	27	Big Gap	do		1				
DODD, John of Wm.					1	Capt. Kelly Co.			
DELL, Joab					1		1		
DELL, Mary	150	Lick Creek	do				2		
EVERHART, David					1				
FARMER, Stephen					1				

87

CAPTAIN HENRY TARRANTS COMPANY 1830

Persons Names	Quantity of Land in Each Tract	Situation or Place Where Each Tract Lies	Material Circumstances of the Title	Common School Lands	No. of White Polls	No. of Town Lots	No. of Slaves	No. of Stud Horses	Pleasure Carriages
GREEN, Jonathan					1				
HENDRY, Joseph	100	Plump	do		1				
HAWKINS, Spears	173	Little Gap	do	160	1				
HARMON, Moses	276	Camp Creek	do	100	1				
HIBARGER, Jacob					1				
JEFFERS, West W.				60	1				
JOHNSON, George					1				
KELLAR, Daniel Sr.	125	Little Gap	do	50					
KELLAR, Daniel Jr.					1				
KELLAR, Benj. Jr.				62½	1				
KELLAR, Benj. Sr.	140	Lick Creek	do	200	1				
KELLAR, Samuel of Benjamin					1				
KELLAR, Jacob					1				
LAEMBAUGH, Daniel	158	Lick Creek	do						
LAEMBAUGH, Fredk.					1				
LAEMBAUGH, Jacob of Jon	100	Dry fork	do	40	1				
LONG, William					1				
MYARS, Michael	100	Gap Creek	do	55					
MARTIN, Daniel	62	Churn Creek	do		1				
MARTIN, James					1				
MORGAN, Jesse				50	1				
McAMIS, James					1				
MONTGOMERY, Letitia	125	Grassy Ck.	do						
McCURRY, Jos. of Is.	20	Plumb Ck.	do	128	1				
McFARLAND, James H	40	Churn Camp	do	60	1				
McFARLAND, And. J.	55	do	do		1				
McKEEHAN, John	55	Churn Camp	do		1				
MYARS, Christr.	30	Gap Creek	do	70	1				
MYARS, Lasley					1				
MURPHEY, Edward	300	Caney Crk.	do	65					
McFARLAND, Andrew	50	Churn Camp	do						
McFARLAND, Hannah of Andrew Sr.				87					
NORTON, Willis					1				
PRICE, John Sr.	300	Punch C.	do	50			3		
PEARCE, James					1				
PARKINS, Elijah					1				
RADANOWERS, John					1				
SPEARS, Eleven				90	1				
SMITH, Thos. Esq.	60	Big Gap	do	16					
SAYLOR, Joseph					1				
SAYLOR, David					1				
SAYLOR, Jacob	50	Plumb	do	343	1				
SAYLOR, Godfrey	278	Chu Can	do	185					
STRONG, William	225	Little Gap	do	48	1				
SMITH, Jacob	317¾	Lick Creek	do		1				
SMITH, Benjamin	67	Campen	do	162					

Persons Names	Quantity of Land in Each Tract	Situation or Place Where Each Tract Lies	Material Circumstances of the Title	Common School Lands	No. of White Polls	No. of Town Lots	No. of Slaves	No. of Stud Horses	Pleasure Carriages
SMITH, George	67	do	do						
SMITH, Frederick	200	Plumb Cr.	do	410	1		1		
SMITH, Robert				640					
SMITH, Beverly	100	Pup C.	do	8	1				
TARRANT, Henry J.	280	Camp C.	do	50	1				
WATTANBARGER, Jac.	150	ditto	do	60	1				
WATTANBARGER, Adam	150	ditto	do	110	1				
WILLIAMS, Joseph	90	ditto	do						
WEST, Wm. Decd. by Administrators	416	B. Gap	do	60					
YOUNG, Frederick					1				
YOUNG, John R.				100	1				
YOUNG, Nancy	200	Lick Gap	do						
		Taken by Frederick SMITH							

Persons Names	Quantity of Land in Each Tract	Situation or Place Where Each Tract Lies	Material Circumstances of the Title	Common School Lands	No. of White Polls	No. of Town Lots	No. of Slaves	No. of Stud Horses	Pleasure Carriages
ANDERSON, Vincent	225	Roaring fk.		50	1		1		
ANDERSON, James	204	do		8	1				
ANDERSON, Benjamin	200	do			1				
ARMITAGE, John	31	do		275	1				
BRITTON, Jas. Mays					1	1			
BROWN, Jotham Sr.	100	do		50	1				
BROWN, Jotham of David	250	do		250	1				
BRITTON, Thomas		do			1				
BRITTON, Wm. Sr.	197	do			1				
BRITTON, Wm. Jr.					1				
BLAIR, William					1				
BLANTON, Absalom	100	do			1				
BUTT, James					1				
BABB, Er. Capt.	86	do		40	1			$1	
BROWN, Silvanus Sr	94	do			1				
BROWN, John					1				
BRANNON, William				25	1				
BROWN, Moses	50	Dry fork			1				
CARTER, Jn. of Jn.	68	Roaring fk.		57	1				
CARTER, Ezekiel of John		do		100	1				
CARTER, Abraham	325	Lick Creek			1				
COOPER, Christr.Jr	80				1				
CARTER, Jacob Jr.					1				
CARTER, Jeol					1				
CARTER, Ezek. Sr.	378	do			1				
CARTER, Elam	64			50	1				
CARTER, Jacob	600	Roaring F.		50	1		1		
CARTER, Benj. Esq.	97½	Dry fork		16	1				
CASTEEL, Jeremiah	108	do		105	1				

Persons Names	Quantity of Land in Each Tract	Situation or Place Where Each Tract Lies	Material Circumstances of the Title	Common School Lands	No. of White Polls	No. of Town Lots	No. of Slaves	No. of Stud Horses	Pleasure Carriages
CAVNER, John	256½	do			1				
CRADDICK, Jesse					1				
CARTER, Mashack					1				
CARTER, John A.		Lick Creek		66	1				
CARTER, Mashec					1	1			
CASTEEL, Peter				100					
COX, Eliakim	152	Roaring F.		330	1				
CATER, William					1				
CASTEEL, Andrew					1				
DELASHMIT, John				50					
DELASHMIT, David				30	1				
DAVIS, Thomas	510	Gass Creek			1		2		
EARNEST, Isaac	1 16/160				1				
EARNEST, H. of Isaac						1			
FOSTER, Robert				25					
FOSTER, Zophar					1				
GASS, John of Jas.	60	do		20	1				
GILLESPIE, Geo. F.	513			155	1	4	6		
GRIMES, James					1				
GASS, Alexander	144	do			1		1		
GASS, H. B.					1		3		
GASS, James	81	Roaring fk.		38					
GASS, Saml. Capt.		do			1				
GASTON, Joseph	142	do		25					
HANKINS, Wm. A.	200	do		100	1		1		
HARDIN, John	245	do		150	1		1	$2	
HATLEY, Sherwood				100	1				
HOLDER, Johnson		Dry fork		100	1				
HANKINS, John E. Heirs	300	do					1		
HARMON, Isaac	313	do		400					
HARMON, Peter	250	do		58	1				
HARMON, John Sr.	367	Gap Creek							
HOPE, Adam					1				
HARMON, Jacob					1				
HOPE, Isaac Jr.					1				
HOPE, Robert					1				
HARMON, John Jr.	275			141	1				
HARMON, Peter Jr.					1				
HOY, John					1	2			
ISBELL, James R.					1	1			
JERMON, William		Dry fork		13	1				
JOHNSTON, Zoph. Jr	65	do		45	1				
JOHNSTON, Joseph					1				
JONES, Thomas					1				
JOHNSTON, Zoph. Sr	198				1				
JOHNSTON, John					1				
KINNEY, James					1				
KOONS, John		do		30	1				
KING, John					1				
KUTON, David					1				

Persons Names	Quantity of Land in Each Tract	Situation or Place Where Each Tract Lies	Material Circumstances of the Title	Common School Lands	No. of White Polls	No. of Town Lots	No. of Slaves	No. of Stud Horses	Pleasure Carriages
KEY, David	324	Roaring fk.		10					
KIDWELL, Elijah		do			1				
KEY, Peter		do			1				
KEY, Daniel		do			1				
KELLER, Samuel	274	do		80	1		1		
KINNEY, John					1				
KIDWELL, Joshua	140								
LUNCH, James Jr.	137½			30	1				
LOGAN, James	100	do			1				
LASHLEY, Alexander		do			1				
LEATHERDELL, John					1				
MELONE, William	209	Dry fork		6					
MELONE, John of Wm		do			1				
MYRICK, Thomas					1				
MELONE, Temprance	240	Lick Creek							
McPHERON, Wm. Sr.	100	Roaring fk.		40					
McPHERON, Jas. Sr.	100	do							
McPHERON, Andrew	150	do			1				
MORRISON, James	131				1				
McPHERON, Elizab.	66								
McKEY, Harmon	28			160					
McCAMIS, Thomas	358	do			1				
McCLENNON, Wm.	26				1	1			
MELONEY, William	200	do			1				
MELONE, Humphrey	111	do			1				
MELONE, West					1				
McCURRY, Samuel					1				
NELSON, Joshua					1				
PITT, Dawson					1				
ROSS, John	215	Lick Creek		50			1		
ROSS, Allen	167	do		6	1				
REDMON, William					1				
RUNELS, David	64	Dry fork		25	1				
RUSSELL, Edwd. Y.	93				1				
RICE, David	386	Roaring fk.		238					
REYNOLDS, Joseph	60	do							
RUSSELL, Elijah	91	do			1				
RHEA, John	50				1	1	3		
REYNOLDS, Clement	19	do		86	1				
REYNOLDS, Jesse	111	Dry fork			1				
ROSS, Wm. of John		do			1				
RUTHERFORD, Ellet				300	1				
STANLEY, William	39			27	1				
SAMPLES, William		Roaring fk.		120	1				
SAMPLES, Robert	143	do		75					
SIMPSON, Henry	125								
SMALL, John					1				
VESTAL, Silas	85	do		70	1		2		
VANCE, Wm. K.	163				1	6	4		
WEEMS, Hannah	600	Lick Creek							
WESTON, Harvey	80				1				
WILSON, John W.	100				1				

CAPTAIN SAMUEL GASS' COMPANY 1830

Persons Names	Quantity of Land in Each Tract	Situation or Place Where Each Tract Lies	Material Circumstances of the Title	Common School Lands	No. of White Polls	No. of Town Lots	No. of Slaves	No. of Stud Horses	Pleasure Carriages
WILSON, Margaret	184								
WELLS, Felix					1				
WEEMS, John of Jas					1				
WEEMS, Jones	205	do		110	1				
WEEMS, John	105	do		65	1		2		
WESTON, John				100	1				
WINKLES, F. T.	100			50					
WEEMS, Geo. Sr.	250	Lick Creek		44			1		
The Same	65								
			By Benjamin CARTER Esqr.						

CAPTAIN GEORGE JENNINGS COMPANY FOR THE YEAR 1830

Persons Names	Quantity of Land in Each Tract	Situation or Place Where Each Tract Lies	Material Circumstances of the Title	Common School Lands	No. of White Polls	No. of Town Lots	No. of Slaves	No. of Stud Horses	Pleasure Carriages
BROYLES, John J.	210	Horse Creek	Deed		1				
BROWN, William	33	do	do						
BIRD, John Junr.	165	do	do		1				
BIRD, John Senr.	127½	do	do						
BITNER, William	142	do	do	20	1				
BURGNER, Elizabeth	188	do	do						
BURGNER, Henry					1				
BRUMLY, David	413	Chucky	do		1		1		
Same	150	Below Town	do						
BELL, George					1				
BROYLES, John Sr.	432½	Horse Creek	do		1				
BROYLES, Zacob	432½	do	do		1		4		
BURDON, James Sr.					1				
BURDON, Stephen					1				
BROYLES, Samuel	160	do	do						
BROYLES, Wm. S.	150	do	do						
BROYLES, John of Michael	85	do	do						
BARNHART, Felix	270	do	do		1				
CANNON, John					1				
EARNEST, Barton	96	L. Sinking	do		1				
EARNEST, Peter	246	Chucky	do				4		
Same	5 7/10	L.S. Creek	do						
EARNEST, Jacob	211	Chucky	do		1		1		
EARNEST, Henry	580	do	do				2		4
EARNEST, Lawrence	112	do	do				1		
EARNEST, Felix Rev	138½	do	do						
Same	89	Sinking Cr.	do						
FOX, Isaac					1				
FULKS, John					1				
FOX, Henry					1				
FOX, Sarah	300	Chucky	do						
FOX, Andrew					1				
FOX, James	255	do	do		1				
FOX, Ezekiel					1				
FELLERS, Abra. G.	400	Chucky	do		1				
Same	150	do	do						

Persons Names	Quantity of Land in Each Tract	Situation or Place Where Each Tract Lies	Material Circumstances of the Title	Common School Lands	No. of White Polls	No. of Town Lots	No. of Slaves	No. of Stud Horses	Pleasure Carriages
Same	133½	Middle Crk.	do						
Same	50	do	do						
GOOD, Manual					1				
GREENE, Ira	125	Chucky	do						
Same	50	do	do						
Same	150	do	do						
Same	100	do	Entry	200					
HISE, James	149	do	deed					1	
HISE, Jacob	200	do	do						
HOYLE, Michael	150	Horse C.	do		1				
HOYLE, Jacob	257	do	do		1				
HAWORTH, Absalom	119	Chucky	do		1			2	
Same	50	do	do						
Same	99	Sinking C.	do						
Same	44½	L. Sinking	do						
JENNINGS, John					1				
JENNINGS, George					1				
JOHNSON, Joseph	50	W. Cart. B.	do		1				
Same	52	Cedar B.	do						
Same	6	L.S. Creek	do						
JOHNSON, Barton	84	Chucky	do		1				
Same for Widow DOBSON	45	do	do		1				
JOHNSON, Henry					1				
KINDLE, William	100	Horse C.	do						
LOTSPEICH, Wm.	206	Chucky	do		1				
MILBURN, John Sr.					1				
MILLER, Adam					1				
MAURIS, Martha	50	do							
MORRISON, Robert					1				
MILLER, George					1				
NEWBERRY, William					1				
NELSON, John					1				
OLIPHANT, Thomas	74	S.C.	Deed						
Same	140	Cedar B.	do						
Same	35	do	do						
PAINTER, Adam	73	Horse C.	do		1				
PAINTHER, Jesse	83	do	do		1				
PRATHAR, Jeremiah					1				1$1
PRATHAR, Delila	130	do	do						
PRATHAR, William	150	do	do		1				
PEARCE, John	150	do	do		1				
PICKERING, Rebecka	160	L.S. Creek	do						
PEARCE, Andrew					1				
PICKERING, John					1				
PICKERING, Jonathn									
RIMELL, Isaac	114	Horse Creek	do		1				
RAMBO, Eli					1				

CAPTAIN GEORGE JENNINGS COMPANY FOR THE YEAR 1830

Persons Names	Quantity of Land in Each Tract	Situation or Place Where Each Tract Lies	Material Circumstances of the Title	Common School Lands	No. of White Polls	No. of Town Lots	No. of Slaves	No. of Stud Horses	Pleasure Carriages
REESER, Daniel					1				
REESER, Jacob	267	Chucky	do						
REESER, John					1				
SEATON, Benjamin	136½	Horse C.	do	100					
SEATON, Moses					1				
STAFFORD, John	151	do	do						
STONECYPHER, Saml.	121	Chucky	do		1				
Same	105¾	Jocky Crk.	do						
SNAPP, John	400	Chucky	do	80	1			1	
WADDELL, Samuel					1				
WILLIAMSON, Jerem.	110	Horse Creek	do		1				
WILLIAMSON, Thomas Revd.				160					
WILLIAMSON, Thomas W.	533	do	do	72	1				
WHITE, Eli	100	Middle C.	do		1				
WHITE, Abraham					1				
WARD, Stephen					1				
		A. G. FELLERS Justice of the P.							

CAPTAIN PARKES COMPANY, JANUARY 16th DAY 1830

Persons Names	Quantity of Land in Each Tract	Situation or Place Where Each Tract Lies	Material Circumstances of the Title	Common School Lands	No. of White Polls	No. of Town Lots	No. of Slaves	No. of Stud Horses	Pleasure Carriages
ALEXANDER, Lorenzo D.					1				
ALEXANDER, Geo. Sr	192	Middle C.	Deed			1			
ALEXANDER, William	180	Chucky			1				
ALEXANDER, Geo. Jr	51	do			1				
BLAKE, Ewen					1				
BOWMAN, Sparling Senr.	532	Camp Creek	do						
BOWMAN, Kennedy					1				
BOWMAN, Jefferson T.					1				
BOWMAN, Benjamin					1				
BOWMAN, Sparling Jr.	104	Camp Creek	do	25	1				
BOWMAN, Aaron					1				
BROYLES, Mary Ann	144	Camp Creek							
CLENDENAN, Jas. A.					1				
COOLEY, Wm. G.					1				
CLICK, John	88	M. C.	do	55	1				
CANNON, Stephen	50	C.C.	do	110	1				
CUMMINS, Philip					1				
CLICK, Malachi	150	Middle C.	do						
The Same	100	Chucky	do						
CLICK, Martin	160	Middle C.	do						
CLICK, George	80	do			1				

Persons Names	Quantity of Land in Each Tract	Situation or Place Where Each Tract Lies	Material Circumstances of the Title	Common School Lands	No. of White Polls	No. of Town Lots	No. of Slaves	No. of Stud Horses	Pleasure Carriages
COTTER, John	26	do	do						
DAVIS, Thomas	143	Camp Creek	do		1				
DAVIS, Elizabeth	382½	Camp Creek	deed	427			5		
FARNSWORTH, David	257	Chucky			1				
FANNON, John					1				
FANNON, Alfred									
HENSHAW, Wash.	185⅛	do	do	5					
HOUSE, George	480	C.C.	do	160					
HOUSE, Washington	40	Camp Creek	do	100					
HOPTON, Aaron	206	Camp Creek	do	54					
HOPTON, Abner					1				
HOPTON, Enoch					1				
HOYLE, Benedict									
HYNSON, Henson D.									
JONES, Geo. Sr.	400	Chucky	Deed				4		
JONES, Balis	612	Camp Creek			1		1		
JENNINGS, James				160	1				
JONES, Thomas	140	Camp Creek	do		1				
JOHNSON, Stephen	241¾	Chucky	do		1				
JOHNSON, William				25					
KENNEDY, John Sr.	227	Camp Creek	do				2		
KENNEDY, Thomas	127½	Chucky					2		
KENNEDY, William					1				
KENNEDY, James P.					1				
KENNEDY, James					1				
KENNEDY, Daniel	68¾	Camp Creek			1				
KERR, William	145	do			1				
KELLY, David					1				
LANEY, John					1				
LANEY, Elizabeth	82	do							
LANEY, Ephraim					1				
LANEY, Jeremiah					1				
LIGHT, John	134½	Camp Creek	do						
LIGHT, Enoch	49	Camp Creek			1				
LIGHT, Obadiah					1				
LEMING, Robert	107				1				
MILLER, Wm. D.	95¼	do	29¼	29¼					
McALPEN, Henry	257	Chucky			1				
McCOY, William					1				
McCORD, John	300	Camp Creek			1				
McAFEE, Archibald	270	do			1				
MUNCHER, John		do		95	1				
MUNCHER, Hagan		do		50					
MORGAN, Josiah		do			1				
NELSON, William	20	Camp Creek			1				
PARK, Enos	55	Chucky	do		1				

Persons Names	Quantity of Land in Each Tract	Situation or Place Where Each Tract Lies	Material Circumstances of the Title	Common School Lands	No. of White Polls	No. of Town Lots	No. of Slaves	No. of Stud Horses	Pleasure Carriages
REAVES, William	75	Camp Creek	do						
REYNOLDS, Henry	569	Camp Creek	do						
SKYLES, John					1				
SMITH, Moses	150	Middle Crk.	Deed	44	1				
SPURGIN, John					1				
SPURGIN, Drury					1				
STOKES, John	10	Middle Crk.		127					
SNAPP, Samuel	421½	Camp Creek	do	210	1		4		
TOW, John					1				
WILHOITE, Samuel	245	Chucky	do						
WILHOITE, John	353	Horse Creek	do		1				
WILHOITE, James	63	Middle Crk.	do	232	1				
WADDLE, Martin	181	Camp Creek	do						
WADDLE, Benjamin	110	do	do		1				
WADDLE, Washington					1				
		Dan KENNEDY J. P.							

CAPTAIN HARRISON'S COMPANY 1830

Persons Names	Quantity of Land in Each Tract	Situation or Place Where Each Tract Lies	Material Circumstances of the Title	Common School Lands	No. of White Polls	No. of Town Lots	No. of Slaves	No. of Stud Horses	Pleasure Carriages
BAILEY, James	471	Camp Creek	Deed						
Same BOWMAN	200	do	do						
BROOKS, Thomas	80	Camp Br.	do		1				
CUTSHALL, Christr.	146	Flag Branch	do	23	1				
CUTSHALL, John	118	do	do	50	1				
CUTSHALL, Fredk. farm CRUMS state	50	do							
DINSMORE, Elizab.	200	Chucky	do				1		
DINSMORE, Leander					1				
DINSMORE, Samuel	100	do	do		1				
DINSMORE, James					1				
DINSMORE, Adam				25	1				
DAVIS, John	187½	Plumb Br.	do						
EVERET, Philip	80	L.S. Creek	deed						
ELISON, John	138	Camp Creek							
FARNSWORTH, Thos.					1				
FARNSWORTH, Robt.	15	Chucky			1				
FARNSWORTH, John Senr.	207	do	do				1		
Same	158								
Same	200								
FARNSWORTH, John Junr.					1				
FRENCH, John P.	217	L.S. Creek	do		1				
FILLERS, Jacob	127	do	do						

Persons Names	Quantity of Land in Each Tract	Situation or Place Where Each Tract Lies	Material Circumstances of the Title	Common School Lands	No. of White Polls	No. of Town Lots	No. of Slaves	No. of Stud Horses	Pleasure Carriages
FILLERS, Michal				74	1				
FILLERS, George					1				
FILLERS, William					1				
FARNSWORTH, Agness	161	Chucky	do				1		
FARNSWORTH, George					1				
GEORGE, Michal	218	Camp Branch	do		1				
HUGHES, Moses	213	L.S. Creek	do	150					
HUGHES, Hezekiah				200	1				
HUGHES, Francis					1				
HUGHES, Aaron					1				
HUGHES, Abraham					1				
HUGHES, George					1				
HARRISON, Jeremiah	232	Dry Branch	do	25	1				
HARRISON, Isaiah	285	Camp Branch	do	25					
Same for T. KELLY estate	133	L.S. Creek	do	3½					
HARRISON, John					1				
HARRISON, Josiah				50	1				
HARRISON, Caleb					1				
HARRISON, William	65	Knobs	do	70	1				
HARRISON, James					1				
JOHNSON, Thomas	100				1				
KELLY, John	100	do	do	222					
Same	45	do	Grant						
KELLY, George	100	Camp Creek			1				
KELLY, Samuel				100	1				
KELLY, Joshua					1				
KELLY, James					1				
KELLY, Jesse	160	do			1				
LITLE, Rebeka	46	L.S. Creek		130					
LENTZ, Jacob	100	do			1				
Same	160	B.L. Creek							
LENTZ, Jonathan	89	L.S. Creek		50	1				
Same				31					
LENTZ, George	156	do			1				
LOTSPEICH, Samuel	200	Chucky			1		3		
McNEW, James				60	1				
McNEW, William	135	Camp Creek		82					
MILLER, John	5	Knobs		25	1				
MILLER, Jacob	60	do		50					
MISSINGER, John					1				
MISSINGER, William	100	Flag Branch	deed	9½	1				
McNEW, Shadrach	57½	do			1				
McNEW, George					1				
REAVES, George	100	Camp Creek			1				
REAVES, Samuel	200	do			1				
RICKER, George	50	L.S. Creek		59	1				
REYNOLDS, Henry Jr					1				

CAPTAIN HARRISON'S COMPANY 1830

Persons Names	Quantity of Land in Each Tract	Situation or Place Where Each Tract Lies	Material Circumstances of the Title	Common School Lands	No. of White Polls	No. of Town Lots	No. of Slaves	No. of Stud Horses	Pleasure Carriages
WOOLSEY, Gilbert Esqr.	249	do		240	1				
Same	126	Chucky							
WOOLSEY, William	395	L.S. Creek	do	260	1				
WOOLSEY, Zephaniah					1				
WILLIAMS, Jas. Jr.	193				1				
WOOLSEY, Zeph. Jr.					1				
WELLS, George	392	L.S. Creek	do	50					
WELLS, Henry					1				
WINTER, Christr.	150	Chucky	do						
WOOLSEY, Thomas					1				
		G. WELLS, Justice							

CAPTAIN PARSON'S COMPANY

Persons Names	Quantity of Land in Each Tract	Situation or Place Where Each Tract Lies	Material Circumstances of the Title	Common School Lands	No. of White Polls	No. of Town Lots	No. of Slaves	No. of Stud Horses	Pleasure Carriages
BRUMLEY, Jacob		Camp Creek			1				
BALEY, James		do		50	1				
BRADY, John		Meadow Crk.			1				
BRADY, Jesse		do			1				
BALL, Lewis	660	Cove Creek					2		
BRUMFIELD, Umphres		Meadow Crk.		75	1				
BIRD, Matthias	147¾	Cove Creek			1				
BIRD, David	240	do		30					
BIRD, Philip H.		do			1				
COOK, John	230	Flag Branch			1				
CRUM, Michal		do			1				
CRUM, Jacob	143	Cove Creek		160	1		1		
CRUM, John Jr.		do		25			1		
CRUM, John Sr.	191	do							
CHAPMAN, William		Meadow Crk.			1				
DANNEL, John		Camp Creek			1				
DUDLEY, Watson	50	do		48					
DUDLEY, Thompson	150	do			1				
DANNEL, Hardin		do			1				
DYKE, Moses					1				
FANN, George	15	Paint Creek			1				
FANN, George Jr.		do		50					
FANN, Frederick					1				
FARNSWORTH, Rebecca	230	Chucky			1		2		
FANN, Solomon	50	Paint Creek			1				
FRESHOUR, George		Cove Creek			1				
FRESHOUR, Joseph		do			1				
FRESHOUR, John Jr.	13¾	Cedar Creek		70	1				
GIBS, Smith		Cove Creek			1				
HAWK, Polser	80½	Cove Creek		16					

Persons Names	Quantity of Land in Each Tract	Situation or Place Where Each Tract Lies	Material Circumstances of the Title	Common School Lands	No. of White Polls	No. of Town Lots	No. of Slaves	No. of Stud Horses	Pleasure Carriages
HAWK, Barnabas		do			1				
HUTCHISON, Joseph	90	do		25	1				
HENDERSON, John Jr		Flag Branch			1				
HOUSTON, William	796½	Cove Creek					5		
HOUSTON, John	437	Cedar Creek					4		
JACK, James	716	Cove Creek							
JACK, Jeremiah	356	Cedar Creek			1				
KELLER, Leonard	37	Cove Creek			1				
KIGER, Peter		do			1				
LOVE, John	192	do			1				
LOTSPEICH, James	312	Cove			1		2		
MIERS, Barnabas	93¾	Cove Creek		100	1				
MYARS, Gabriel		C. Creek			1				
MISEMORE, Peter	190	do			1				
MORGAN, Thomas	75	do							
PARMAN, Emanuel	520	Flag Branch							
PETERS, Jacob		M. Creek			1				
PETERS, Abraham	367	Meadow Crk.							
PARMAN, John	167½	Flag Branch			1				
PETERS, Abraham	420	Meadow Crk.		70					
PARSONS, John	60	Cove Creek		157	1				
ROSE, Alexander		Cedar Creek		40	1				
RICOR, Frederick	175				1				
RICOR, John	83				1				
ROBERTS, Jeremiah		Cove Creek			1				
ROLLINGS, William	20	do			1				
ROLLINGS, Nancy	91	do							
RICOR, Jacob	18	Paint Creek		57					
RICOR, Martin		do		85	1				
RICOR, Gideon		Cove Creek			1				
REYNOLDS, Thomas		Brush Creek			1				
REYNOLDS, William	58	Paint Creek		325					
REATHER, Jacob	125			50	1				
REYNOLDS, Stephen		do		50	1				
STEPHENS, Andrew	400	Cove Creek		2½	1		4		
SMEATHERS, Philip	50	do		25	1				
St JOHN, Zephaniah	71	Brush Creek		205	1				
St JOHN, William		do			1				
SMEATHERS, John		Cove Creek			1				
SMEATHERS, Phil Sr	262	do							
SMEATHERS, George	38				1				
STEPHENS, Samuel		do			1				
St JOHN, Job		Brush Creek			1				
TUCKER, James		Cedar Creek		50					
TALTON, William		Cove Creek			1				
VARNER, William	60	do			1				

Persons Names	Quantity of Land in Each Tract	Situation or Place Where Each Tract Lies	Material Circumstances of the Title	Common School Lands	No. of White Polls	No. of Town Lots	No. of Slaves	No. of Stud Horses	Pleasure Carriages
WILLHOITE, Samuel		Flag Branch			1				
WILLHOITE, John	453	Cove Creek		98	1			1	$1.50
WILLHOITE, William									
WILLIS, John	101	Meadow Crk.							
WILLHOITE, Sol. Jr		Cove Creek			1				
WILLHOITE, Simeon		Flag Branch			1				
WILLET, Joshua		Paint Creek		72	1				
WELLS, Humphreys	44	Cove Creek		17	1				
WELLS, Jacob		do			1				
		By T. BALL, J. P.							

CAPTAIN OTTINGER'S COMPANY 1830

Persons Names	Quantity of Land in Each Tract	Situation or Place Where Each Tract Lies	Material Circumstances of the Title	Common School Lands	No. of White Polls	No. of Town Lots	No. of Slaves	No. of Stud Horses	Pleasure Carriages
BUSLER, Christian	150	Slate Creek	deed						
BOWERS, John	300	M. Creek	ditto						
BUSTER, Archibald	25	ditto	ditto	275	1				
BUSTER, William					1				
BUSTER, John					1	1			
BYERS, Chas. P.					1				
BELL, Joseph E.	105	C. Branch	do	30	1				
BUSTER, Michael, Adr. Dd.									
BROWNING, Benj. D.				82½					
BROWNING, Rebeca	62	M. Creek	Ditto						
CANNON, James					1				
COOK, George	212¾	C. Branch	ditto						
CANNON, John	300	C. River	ditto		1				
COCHRAN, Samuel	100	F. Branch			1				
CUNINGHAM, John					1				
COGGBURN, John									
CRAWFORD, Wm. M.	200	M. Creek	ditto	120	1		1	1	$3
CRAWFORD, Isbel							3		
CALLIHAN, James					1				
EBERLY, John				100	1				
EASTERLY, Abraham	16	C. River	do						
EASTERLY, Philip	121	C. River	do						
EASTERLY, Jac. Sr.	99	C. River	do						
EASTERLY, George	216	C. River	ditto		1				
EASTERLY, Jacob	70	C. River	ditto	16	1				
FORBEA, Jacob	172	C. River	ditto						
GRAGG, John	300	C. Branch	ditto	50					
GRAGG, William	265	C. Branch	ditto	140					
GRAGG, Robert	7	C. Branch	ditto	25	1				
GRAGG, Geo. M.					1				
GAMMONS, Ivy	4	O. Creek	ditto	100	1				
GAMMONS, Henry					1				
GABLE, Barnabas	125	M. Creek	ditto	5					

Persons Names	Quantity of Land in Each Tract	Situation or Place Where Each Tract Lies	Material Circumstances of the Title	Common School Lands	No. of White Polls	No. of Town Lots	No. of Slaves	No. of Stud Horses	Pleasure Carriages
HENDERSON, Samuel	158	C. River	ditto	100	1				
HENDERSON, John	180	C. Branch	ditto	60					
HENDERSON, John	399¼	C. River	ditto	150	1		2		
HENKLE, Philip	103	M. Creek	ditto	329					
HENDERSON, Joseph					1				
HENDERSON, Charles					1				
HALE, Joseph					1				
HENKEL, Irenius									
KYKER, John	200	C. River	ditto	32					
KELLY, Jacob					1				
LINBARGER, Chas.	64	M. Creek	ditto		1				
McMURTREY, James	330	C. Branch	ditto	265			6	1	$4
McKENNY, Saml. S.	490	C.B. dit	ditto						
McKEMY, Robert	27	ditto	ditto	45	1				
McKEMY, Alexander					1				
McALISTER, John	400	C. River	ditto						
MASNER, George	245	C. R.							
McMURTREY, John	86	C. B.	ditto	25	1				
MASNER, Peter					1				
McCOY, William					1				
McCOY, John					1				
MASNER, Peter Sr.	150	C. River	ditto		1				
MIMMS, Alfred	77	S. Creek	ditto						
NEESE, John Sr.	243	M. Creek	ditto		1				
NEESE, John	574	ditto	ditto	150	1				
NEESE, Adam	200	ditto	ditto		1				
NEILSON, Arch.	460	C. River	ditto	135	1		5		
NEESE, George	300	C. Branch	ditto	71					
NEESE, Philip	423	R. Spring		50					
NEESE, Abraham					1				
NEESE, Samuel					1				
OTTINGER, Jonas	86	C. Branch	ditto		1				
OTTINGER, Jacob	125	M. C.	ditto	55	1				
OTTINGER, John Jr.	200	S. C.	ditto	56	1				
OTTINGER, John Sr.	500	S. C.	ditto	56			2		
OTTINGER, Peter					1				
OTTINGER, William					1				
OTTINGER, Lewis	182	C. B.	ditto						
PETER, John	85	C. B.	dit	75	1				
PETERS, Abraham									
PETERS, Jacob									
RENNER, John	150	M. Creek	Deed	50	1				
RENNER, John Sr.	717	ditto	ditto	200					
REASE, John	175	C. River			2				
ROBERTS, Berry									
REASE, William									
RENNER, Michael					1				
RENNER, Joseph					1				
RHINEHART, Geo.	32	M. Creek	Bond						

Persons Names	Quantity of Land in Each Tract	Situation or Place Where Each Tract Lies	Material Circumstances of the Title	Common School Lands	No. of White Polls	No. of Town Lots	No. of Slaves	No. of Stud Horses	Pleasure Carriages
STINE, John	70	S. Creek	Deed						
STINE, Andrew	90	dit	dit	90	1				
SMITH, Reuben	43	C. B.	dit	65	1				
SMITH, James	250	C. River		50					
SHERLY, Isaac					1				
STEPHENS, Andrew	140	C. River	do		1		2	1	$4
SHERLY, Nathan					1				
SHIRLEY, John					1				
STUART, William					1				
TOBY, Henry				218	1				
WHITTENBURG, Jac.					1	1			
WOODS, Michael	900	M. Creek	deed	50					
WELTY, John	101	M. Creek	do						

By Wm. M. CRAWFORD, Justice of the Peace

Persons Names	Quantity of Land in Each Tract	Situation or Place Where Each Tract Lies	Material Circumstances of the Title	Common School Lands	No. of White Polls	No. of Town Lots	No. of Slaves	No. of Stud Horses	Pleasure Carriages
ALEXANDER, George	63	C. R.	D		1				
ALLEN, Daniel	1166	C. R.	D	50	1		6		
ALLEN, Samuel	480	do	D		1		4		
BASINGER, Jacob	10	P. C.	D		1				
BELL, George					1				
BASINGER, Mich. Jr	120	P. C.	D		1				
BASINGER, Philip	116	do	D		1				
BROOKS, Jacob					1				
BASINGER, Jacob					1				
BASING, Michael	137	do	D						
BROOKS, Stephen	391	C. R.	D						
CRAIG, Jane	400	R. S. C.	D						
CRAIG, John					1				
CHAMPLAIN, James					1				
DEWIT, Frances	80	C. R.	D				2		
DUNLAP, William	100	L. C. C.	D		1				
DUNLAP, John	150	C. R.	D		1				
DEARSTONE, Mich.	514	P. C.	D	150	1				
DEARSTONE, Abraham					1				
DEARSTONE, Isaac					1				
DEARSTONE, Jacob					1				
DYKE, Henry Sr.	385	L. S. P.	D						
DYKE, Henry Jr.					1				
DYKE, Alex.					1				
DYKE, Jacob	930	C. R.	D		1		1		
DUNLAP, John for Geo. COCHRAN dd.	400	C. R.	D						
EALY, Adam	370	P. C.	D		1				

Persons Names	Quantity of Land in Each Tract	Situation or Place Where Each Tract Lies	Material Circumstances of the Title	Common School Lands	No. of White Polls	No. of Town Lots	No. of Slaves	No. of Stud Horses	Pleasure Carriages
FARNSWORTH, David	631	R. L. C.	D				1		
FARNSWORTH, Henry	100	C. R.	D						
FARNSWORTH, Jere.	190	R. L. C.	D		1				
FARNER, Jacob	47	P. C.	D						
FEEZEL, Henry	650	do	D		1				
FARNSWORTH, Thos.	147	C. R.	D		1				
FARNSWORTH, Allen					1				
GOOD, David	320	C. R.	D		1				
GLASS, John	57	R. D. C.	D						
GUIN, James					1				
GARDNER, Conrad	200	do	D		1				
GIBSON, John					1				
GRIMES, William					1				
GUIN, Rachel	225	P. D.	D						
GLASS, James					1				
GRIMES, John	121	do	D	55	1				
GEORGE, William	163	C. R.	D		1				
HYBARGER, Joseph					1				
HALL, William	477	R. L. C.	D	10			1		
HALL, Alexander					1				
JEFFERS, Franky	28	R. L. C.	D						
JONES, Phineas	505	do	D						
The Same John									
JONES, Decd.	218	F. L. C.	D						
LAUDERDALE, James	190	C. R.	D		1				
McBRIDE, William	161½	P. C.	D						
McALPIN, John					1				
McCAMISH, Thomas	60	R. L. C.	D						
McKEEHAN, Samuel	30	do	D		1				
McKEEHAN, John	90½	do	D						
McKEEHAN, James	100	do	D		1				
MARTIN, William	110	C. R.	D		1			1 $1¼	
MAXWELL, Moses	178	P. C.	D		1				
McGILL, Hugh	200		D						
McBRIDE, James	253½	L. Ck.	D		1				
McBRIDE, Martin	230	L. C.	D		1				
PETERS, Isaac					1				
PETERS, Elizabeth	100	P. C.	D						
PEARCE, James	207	C. R.	D		1				
RECTOR, John	155	L. C. C.	D						
RECTOR, John S.					1				
RUSSELL, David	125	P. C.	D		1				
ROBERTS, John	64	do	D		1				
ROBERTS, James				55	1				
SWATZIL, Henry	200	P. C.	D		1				
SWATZIL, Jacob					1				
SWATZIL, Polly	20	R. L. C.	D						
SHARP, William	32½	do	D	10					

CAPTAIN SUSONG'S COMPANY 1830

Persons Names	Quantity of Land in Each Tract	Situation or Place Where Each Tract Lies	Material Circumstances of the Title	Common School Lands	No. of White Polls	No. of Town Lots	No. of Slaves	No. of Stud Horses	Pleasure Carriages
SWATZIL, Philip	138	do	D						
SWATZIL, Henry					1				
SUSONG, Alexander	33	P. C.	D		1				
SUSONG, Elizabeth	106	do	D						
SUSONG, Andw. Jr.	161	C. R.	D		1		1		
SUSONG, Andw. Sr.	214	C. R.	D		1				
SUSONG, John	115	do	D		1				
SMELSER, Jacob	20	L. C.	D		1				
SWATZIL, Jac. Sr.	200	P. C.	D		1				
SUSONG, Alfred					1				
TEMPLE, Polly	240	R. L. C.	D				2		
THOMPSON, Henry	250	C. R.	D						
WOOLSEY, William	33	C. R.	D		1				
WILLHOIT, Philip	165	R. L. C.	D		1			1 $1	
WILSON, Hugh	80	do	D		1				
WILSON, Ephraim	132	do	D		1				
WEAVER, Frederick	151	P. C.	D						
WRIGHT, John	101	R. L. C.	D		1				
WOOLHAVER, Philip Sr.	265½	P. C.	D						
WOOLHAVER, Philip Jr.	87½	P. C.	D		1				
WHITTENBURG, Peter	350	R. L. C.	D	50	1				
WYKLE, William	121	do	D						

By J. FARNSWORTH, J. P.

CAPTAIN LAUGHNER'S COMPANY 1830

Persons Names	Quantity of Land in Each Tract	Situation or Place Where Each Tract Lies	Material Circumstances of the Title	Common School Lands	No. of White Polls	No. of Town Lots	No. of Slaves	No. of Stud Horses	Pleasure Carriages
ANDERS, George	428	L. Chucky					1		
ANDREWS, Andrew					1				
ABEL, Jonathan	129				1				
BAUHERD, John	150				1				
BAUHERD, Jacob				25	1				
BAUHERD, William	85				1				
COBBLE, John	250			100	1				
COBBLE, Adam	100				1				
CLARY, Zacki	50				1				
DUNLAP, Joseph	110½				1				
DUNWOODY, William	200			50	1				
DUNWOODY, P. M.	100			50	1				
DUNWOODY, John	100			50	1				
EGLE, William					1				
ELEY, Nicholas	160				1				
ETTER, Fred. W.					1				

Persons Names	Quantity of Land in Each Tract	Situation or Place Where Each Tract Lies	Material Circumstances of the Title	Common School Lands	No. of White Polls	No. of Town Lots	No. of Slaves	No. of Stud Horses	Pleasure Carriages
FRY, James					1				
FRY, George					1				
GUIN, Robert					1				
GREENLEE, Mannon					1				
GOOD, John	222				1				
HENDERSON, John	200			20	1				
HUFF, Elias	100								
HUFF, Jacob					1				
HARMON, Christian	245								
HARMON, John					1				
JOHNSON, Richard	67				1				
KERBY, Jesse	360	Lick Creek			1				
KETTENING, Val.	140				1				
KING, George	328	L. Creek							
KING, Stephen					1				
KISLING, John	290				1				
KINSER, Henry					1				
LAMB, Marmaduke	25				1				
LAUGHNER, Christn.	105			54					
LAUGHNER, Daniel	44			100	1				
LONES, Adam	270			154					
LONES, George	100			100	1				
RADER, William	100				1				
RANKIN, Anthony	135				1				
SMILEY, Andrew	317				1				
SMELCER, Henry	208				1				
SMITH, Susan	88			50					
SMITH, Daniel					1				
SMITH, James	69			100	1				
TROBAUGH, George	75			120	1				
TROBAUGH, William					1				
TROBAUGH, Samuel					1				
TROBAUGH, Freder.	464			116				1	
WELTY, Martin	150				1				
WAMPLER, Solomon				140	1				
WAMPLER, Ben	50			100	1				
WAMPLER, Fred	15				1				

By Anthy. RANKIN, Esqr.

Persons Names	Quantity of Land in Each Tract	Situation or Place Where Each Tract Lies	Material Circumstances of the Title	Common School Lands	No. of White Polls	No. of Town Lots	No. of Slaves	No. of Stud Horses	Pleasure Carriages
ADAMS, John	40	W. L. C.			1				
BURKEY, Polly	130	W. L. Ck.	Deed	29					
BROWN, Joseph	133	Dr. R.L. Ck.	Grant			3			
BROWN, John A.	71	W.R.L. Cr.	Deed		1				
BRITTON, J. Daniel	130	W.L. Creek	do		1				
BAILS, William	207	ditto		50	1				
BOYLES, John	15	ditto		80					
BOYLES, George					1				
BROWN, Geo. Alex.	200	W. Cove Ck.			2	4			
Ditto	300	W.L. Ck.							
Ditto	30	W.R.L. Cr.							
Ditto	75	D.H. Cr.							
Ditto	78	Greeneville							
Ditto	360	W.L. Ck.							
CARBAUGH, George					1				
CARBAUGH, Jacob				10	1				
CARBAUGH, John	150	W.L. Ck.	Deed	32½	1				
CARVER, George					1				
CARBAUGH, Daniel	25	W.L. Ck.	do	195	1				
COPICK, Abraham					1				
COTTER, Joseph					1		1		
DYKE, Emanuel	48	W.L. Ck.		52	1				
DYCHE, Christian	58			71	1				
DYCHE, Michael				29	1				
DYCHE, John									
DAVIS, John (stranger)					1				
DICKSON, William	2538	W.R.L. Ck.			1	7	10		
DYCHE, Hirmonous	60			41	1				
DAVIS, Thomas	401	W.L. Ck.			1		2		
DICKSON, John	131	R.L.C.	Deed		1	4	3		1 2W
DOBSON, Robert	143	W.L. Cr.							
EASTERLY, Casper	180	L. Ck.	Deed		1				
EVANS, William	268	W.L. Ck.		152	1		1		
FARNER, Jacob					1				
FRENCH, Henry					1				
GUIN, John	100				1	1			
GASS, Charles	150	W.L. Cr.			1				
GAMBLE									
HULL, John Senr.	394	W.L. Ck.							
HULL, Jacob					1				
HULL, John Junr.					1				
HARMON, John	275	W.L. Cr.		141	1	(see Gass' Co)			
HARTMAN, Marshel	117	L. Ck.	Deed	93	1				
JOHNSTON, Andrew									
JONES, George	6½				1	1	2		
JOHNSTON, James					1				

Persons Names	Quantity of Land in Each Tract	Situation or Place Where Each Tract Lies	Material Circumstances of the Title	Common School Lands	No. of White Polls	No. of Town Lots	No. of Slaves	No. of Stud Horses	Pleasure Carriages
KINCANNON, S. A.					1				
KENNEDY, Andrew & James									
LYNCH, James	38	W.L. Cr.		137	1	(see Gass' Co)			
LYSTER, John					1				
LAMB, M. Duke	25				1	1			
LAUGHLIN, W. K.					1				
LEMING, Robert	77	W.L. Ck.		140	(see Parks Co.)				
MYERS, Henry	212½	W.L. Ck.		4					
MITCHELL, Thos. Sr	158	ditto							
MITCHELL, Thos. Jr					1				
MITCHELL, John					1				
McAMISH, Robert					1				
MORRISS, John					1				
MALONEY, Robert					1		2		
MALONEY, John				100	1				
PROFFIT, Adam	230			54	1				
PATTERSON, James	400					2	1		
PARK, Andrew Jr.					1				
PARK, Alexander					1				
PARK, Andrew Sr.	5	Greeneville							
PERRY, Wm. S.					1	1			
RHEA, John (Honbl)	400	W.L. Cr.				2			
RUSSELL, Robert	300	W.L. Ck.							
RUSSELL, Alfred					1				
RUSSELL, Jane	640				4	1			
REYNOLDS, Vincent					1				
REED, Andrew	100	W.L. Cr.							
SMITHERS, Thomas					1				
SIPE, Benjamin				50	1				
SMELSER, George	10	W. Creek	D	100	1				
TROBAUGH, George	165	W.L. Ck.	D	84	1				
TROBAUGH, Jacob					1				
TROBAUGH, Daniel	164	W.L. Ck.			1				
VANCE, James	100	W.L. Cr.			1				
VESTAL, William					1				
WYLY, Martin	150	W.L. Ck.			1				
WILLIAMS, Alexr.	177				1	4	8		1-4W
WOODS, R. M.	73½				1	1	1		
YOUNG, Darius					1				

By Jos. BROWN, J. P.

Persons Names	Quantity of Land in Each Tract	Situation or Place Where Each Tract Lies	Material Circumstances of the Title	Common School Lands	No. of White Polls	No. of Town Lots	No. of Slaves	No. of Stud Horses	Pleasure Carriages
AYRES, Samuel	200	L.C.	Deed		1				
ABEL, Jonathan	125	do	do		1				
ANDERS, Adam	150	do	do						
AARON, Abraham					1				
BIBLE, Jonathan					1				
BIBLE, John	150	do	do	29					
BIBLE, Christn. Sr	160	do	do						
BIBLE, Lewis	100	do	do						
BIBLE, Abraham					1				
BIBLE, Christn. Jr	80				1				
BIBLE, Jacob	93			14	1				
BEWLY, Anthy. Jr.	214	do	do		1				
BEWLY, Jacob M.	200	B.C.	do	200	1		2		
BROWN, Isaac	160	L.C.	do		1				
BROWN, David					1				
BROWN, Abraham					1				
BROWN, John					1				
BOWERS, Moses	145				1				
BAKER, William					1				
BAKER, Allen					1				
BRYAN, Daniel	550				1		3		
BIBLE, Adam	200				1				
BYOYLES, Cyrus					1				
BIBLE, Philip	450								
COX, Matthew					1				
CURTON, Richard	89½	B.C.			1		3		
CURTON, Thomas					1				
COFFMAN, Daniel	260						2		
DYER, Samuel					1				
HALE, Hugh D.	930	B.C.			1	10			
HARRISON, Sol	30	L.C.			1				
HARRISON, Josiah					1				
KIRK, Barbary	150	L.C.							
KIRK, John					1				
KIRK, James					1				
LEMMONS, John					1				
MALONEY, Hugh	240	B.C.			1				
McLAIN, Thomas					1				
NIP, Varnon	90	do	do						
NIP, Daniel	160	do	do		1				
NIP, Christian	146	do	do						
POE, William	1½	W.B.			1				
PERDEE, James					1				
PITSBERGER, John	105	S.C.			1				
RAGAN, Robert	150	B.C.			1				
REED, David	154	L.C.			1			$2	

CAPTAIN REED'S COMPANY 1830

Persons Names	Quantity of Land in Each Tract	Situation or Place Where Each Tract Lies	Material Circumstances of the Title	Common School Lands	No. of White Polls	No. of Town Lots	No. of Slaves	No. of Stud Horses	Pleasure Carriages
RANKIN, William	175	do							
RANKIN, David					1				
STULTS, Lewis	163	do							
STULTS, John					1				
SMITH, William	422	S.C.			1		1		
SMITH, Robert	100	do							
SCRUGGS, Richard	1012	B.C.					7		
SCRUGGS, James	35	W.B.			1		4		
SCRUGGS, Abijah					1				
SCRUGGS, Rufus					1				
SCRUGGS, William	225	B.C.							
SCRUGGS, Wm. Jr.					1				
SEVIER, James					1				
SCULLY, William					1				
SMITH, Charles					1				
THOMPSON, Elijah					1				
THOMPSON, James					1				
TAYLOR, Lewis					1				
TAYLOR, Simeon					1				
VOYLES, Robert					1				
WYSCOVER, William					1				
WILLIAMS, James					1				
WATES, David					1				
		By J. M. BEWLY, J. P.							

CAPTAIN McPHERON'S COMPANY 1830

Persons Names	Quantity of Land in Each Tract	Situation or Place Where Each Tract Lies	Material Circumstances of the Title	Common School Lands	No. of White Polls	No. of Town Lots	No. of Slaves	No. of Stud Horses	Pleasure Carriages
ALTUM, James					1				
BLACK, Wm. Decd.	250	Lick Creek	Deed						
BLACK, Joseph	115		do						
BROWN, David	105	Gap Creek	do	100	1				
BOIÑ, Abraham	250		do	400	1				
BLAKELY, John	95		do		1				
BROWN, Thomas	25	Lick Creek	Deed	75					
BURKET, Isaac					1				
BARNES, James					1				
BARNES, Wesley					1				
BROWN, David	25		do	75	1				
BIBLE, George	334	do	do		1				
BIBLE, Isaac	100		do		1				
COBBLE, Peter	240	do	do		1				
COBBLE, Philip	93		do		1				
COBBLE, Jacob	142½		do		1				
DRAKE, Gabriel	150	Stoney Ck.	do	100					

Persons Names	Quantity of Land in Each Tract	Situation or Place Where Each Tract Lies	Material Circumstances of the Title	Common School Lands	No. of White Polls	No. of Town Lots	No. of Slaves	No. of Stud Horses	Pleasure Carriages
DAVIS, Paul					1				
ETTER, John	321	Lick Creek	do						
ETTER, William	165		do		1				
ETTER, Jefferson	95		do		1				
EPLEY, Daniel				100					
FRY, John Decd.	530	do							
FRY, Philip					1				
FRY, Christopher					1				
FRY, Henry	126	do			1				
FRY, George	100	do			1				
FOSTER, R. S.					1				
GLASCOCK, George					1				
GLASCOCK, Geo. Dd.	346	do	do						
GLASCOCK, John	162	do	do				1		
GLASCOCK, Jesse					1				
GUTHRIE, Jas. Dd.	530	do					4		
GUTHRIE, Andrew					1				
GREEN, Thomas					1		1		
HARMON, Jacob	72	do							
HARMON, Philip	507	Little C.			1				
HUNTER, John	200	Lick Creek	do		1				
HUNTER, Thomas	104	Grassy Ck.	do						
HUNTER, Mary	100	do							
HALL, Wilson					1				
HILL, M. W.					1				
INGLEDOVE, Wm. Jr.				50	1				
INGLEDOVE, John									
INGLEDOVE, Wm. Sr.	25								
JACKSON, George					1				
JACKSON, Thomas					1				
JACKSON, Vincent	290	Lick Creek					1		
JOHNSON, James					1				
JERAEL, Benjamin					1				
KIRKPATRICK	160	Black C.	Deed						
KENSOR, George	130				1				
KENSOR, Jacob	180	Lick Creek			1				
KIKER, Jacob					1				
KINSOR, Adam	185	Lick Creek			1				
KATRON, Jacob	125								
LAUGHNER, John	74	do	do		1				
LADY, John	230	do	do		1				
LADY, William	105								
LOWRY, Alexander					1				
LOWRY, Charles					1				
MORGAN, Lewis					1				
MILLER, Christr.				100					
McCOLLOUGH, Wm.	122			200	1				

CAPTAIN McPHERON'S COMPANY 1830

Persons Names	Quantity of Land in Each Tract	Situation or Place Where Each Tract Lies	Material Circumstances of the Title	Common School Lands	No. of White Polls	No. of Town Lots	No. of Slaves	No. of Stud Horses	Pleasure Carriages
MYERS, Nancy	164								
McPHERON, Andrew				300	1				
McPHERON, Susan	180								
MISEMER, Mary	435								
MASE, Ann	66								
MASE, John	60								
MURRAY, Reuben	217				1	1			
MASE, David					1				
MASE, Henry	77			200	1				
MASE, Nicholas	160				1				
PHILIPS, Thomas	170				1				
PETTIT, Nenemiah	120				1				
RADER, Gasper	30			170	1				
RADER, Joseph	170				1				
RADER, Jesse	137½				1				
RADER, William	124				1				
RADER, John Junr.	50				1				
RADER, Elizabeth	172								
RADER, Henry	240						1		
RADER, Martin	120½								
RADER, Daniel					1				
RADER, John	106								
SCOTT, John	50			137	1				
SCOTT, James	140				1				
SHARP, William					1				
SHIELDS, James	282						1		
SELF, Thomas	660	Lick Creek		300					Carriage
SELF, Clabourn	97	Gap Creek			1				
SHAVOR, Henry					1				
SIPE, Henry	225								
SMITH, Ezekiel	111				1				
SHAVER, Frederick	100								
TROBAUGH, William	110			53					
TROBAUGH, Myers					1				
VANSKILE, Aaron									
WILLOUGHBY, Wm.	120			200	1	(Gass Co. decd.)			
WILLOUGHBY, John	10			200	1				
WILLOUGHBY, Mary	226½	Gap Creek							
WILSON, Thomas	100				1				
WILSON, Moses	125	Lick Creek	deed		1				

By Jesse KIRBY, Justice of the Peace

Persons Names	Quantity of Land in Each Tract	Situation or Place Where Each Tract Lies	Material Circumstances of the Title	Common School Lands	No. of White Polls	No. of Town Lots	No. of Slaves	No. of Stud Horses	Pleasure Carriages
ADAMS, Thomas	50	Lick Creek	D		1				
ADAMS, Thomas					1				
BROTHERTON, Bn.	103	Lick	Deed		1				
BRAGG, William				162					
BRAGG, Ephraim				73	1				
BRAGG, Andrew					1				
BROTHERTON, James					1				
BROTHERTON, Ben					1				
COUCH, John Sr.	416	Gap Creek	D	210					
CARTER, Ellis	214	L.C.	D	100	1				
CARTER, Barton					1				
FRAZIER, Thomas	150	Lick	D					1	
FRAZIER, David	109	do	D		1				
FRAZIER, Johnson					1				
FRAZIER, George	250	do	Deed		1				
FIELDS, Lansford				170	1				
FRAZIER, Isaac				100					
GOODIN, Ben	138½		D		1				
GOODIN, James	350								
HODGES, Samuel				150					
HOWEL, Joseph					1				
HARTLEY, Daniel	40	Gr. C.	D	85	1				
HAIL, Jesse M.					1				
HARDE, Elijah					1				
JONES, Lewis	72	L.C.	D		1				
JONES, Samuel	185	do	D						
JONES, Wm. Sr.	205	S. Cr.	D	40					
JONES, Wm. Jr.					1				
JONES, Samuel H.					1				
LINDSAY, Elizabeth	194	Ga.	D					1	
MEDLY, Bryant					1				
MYERS, John	100	G.C.	D	50					
MYERS, Christr.					1				
McDANEL, John	100	G.C.	D		1				
MERREMAN, William					1				
MANES, Stephen				100	1				
NICHOLS, Charles	95	Snow Creek	D		1				
POGUE, Farmer	168	Gap Creek	Deed	120	1				
PAYNE, Chesley					1				
PAYNE, William				100	1				
PRATT, Constant	30	L.C.	D	106	1				
PRATT, Robert					1				
PRATT, Alexander					1				
POGUE, William	100				1				
RUTHERFORD, Ben					1				

CAPTAIN JONES' COMPANY

Persons Names	Quantity of Land in Each Tract	Situation or Place Where Each Tract Lies	Material Circumstances of the Title	Common School Lands	No. of White Polls	No. of Town Lots	No. of Slaves	No. of Stud Horses	Pleasure Carriages
RUDDING, Alexr.					1				
RUSSELL, Joseph	37	L							
RUTHERFORD, Ruha	75	G.C.	Deed						
RICKETS, Brazillai	100	Snow Camp	D		1				
RINKER, Philip	100	L.C.	D						
The Same	300								
REDMON, William					1				
STOUT, Peter	150	L.C.	D						
SHELLY, James	73	G.C.	D						
SWEET, Isaac					1				
SMILEY, Walter	90	L.C.	D		1				
STOUT, Jesse					1				
VARNUM, Elizabeth				40					
WALKER, Isaac					1				
WILLIAMS, Bn.	273	Li. Cr.	D	210	1				
WILLIAMS, Ira					1				
WEEMS, Geo. Jr.	617	Li. Cr.	D		1				
WEST, Reuben					1				
WEEMS, Abraham	130	Pun Camp	D		1				
WELLS, Israel					1				

By Wm. JONES, Justice of the Peace

CAPTAIN COOK'S COMPANY 1830

Persons Names	Quantity of Land in Each Tract	Situation or Place Where Each Tract Lies	Material Circumstances of the Title	Common School Lands	No. of White Polls	No. of Town Lots	No. of Slaves	No. of Stud Horses	Pleasure Carriages
BOULS, Elizabeth	155		D						
BIGGS, James	210				1	1			
BOWERS, Christian	400								
BOWERS, Joel					1				
BROWN, Guthrie	761				2		5	1	$2.50
BAKER, Peter	75								
BIBLE, Jacob	68				1				
COCHRAN, Robert					1				
COOK, Christopher					1				
EVINS, Even	200				1				
EVANS, Robert	325				1	1			
EVANS, Hannah	136¾								
HUFF, Elias Jr.					1				
HALL, Alexander	176				1	1			
HENEGAR, Henry	230				1				
HUFF, Joseph	150			50	1				
HENRY, James	148				1				
HENKEL, Samuel					1				
HARRISON, Jesse					1				
KIFER, John	154¾								

Persons Names	Quantity of Land in Each Tract	Situation or Place Where Each Tract Lies	Material Circumstances of the Title	Common School Lands	No. of White Polls	No. of Town Lots	No. of Slaves	No. of Stud Horses	Pleasure Carriages
LOVE, Nancy	171						1		
LOVE, John	300						2		
LOVE, John T.	120	Chucky					2		
MAGILL, Thomas	100				1				
MAGILL, James	200								
MAGILL, Harvy	60				1				
MAGILL, John					1				
MAGILL, Hugh M.					1				
MAGILL, Samuel	100			16	1				
MAGILL, Isaac N.					1				
MALONEY, Robert	10			200	1	2			
MALONEY, John					1				
RUSSELL, Hezekiah	145			30				1 $2	
RUSSELL, William	50				1				
RUSSELL, Arch.					1				
RUSSELL, John					1				
RINEHART, Jacob	176			10	1				
SNIDER, Abraham	130								
SNIDER, Jacob					1				
STONE, John	70				1				
SMELSER, Joseph	100				1				
SNIDER, David					1				
SHEFFEY, John					1				
SHAM, James					1				
SHIELDS, John	100			50	1				
SHIELDS, William					1				
SHIELDS, Esther	250			50					
WHITTENBURG, Wm.	585								
WHITTENBURG, John					1				
WHITTENBURG, Moses					1				
WILSON, Adam	200				1				
WHEELER, Saml. A.	1000				1				
		By Henry DYCHE, J. P.							

Persons Names	Quantity of Land in Each Tract	Situation or Place Where Each Tract Lies	Material Circumstances of the Title	Common School Lands	No. of White Polls	No. of Town Lots	No. of Slaves	No. of Stud Horses	Pleasure Carriages
BLACK, James									
BLACK, Joseph									
BOWLING, Josh. Sr.	100	L.C.	Deed						
BRYAN, John Sr.	208	L.C.							
BOWLING, Josh. Jr.					1				
BOWLING, William									
BRYAN, Elizabeth	200	W.L.C.							
BLACK, Elizabeth	170	B.C.							
BEWLY, John									
BEWLY, Anthony									
BLACK, John					1				

CAPTAIN DAVIS' COMPANY 1830

Persons Names	Quantity of Land in Each Tract	Situation or Place Where Each Tract Lies	Material Circumstances of the Title	Common School Lands	No. of White Polls	No. of Town Lots	No. of Slaves	No. of Stud Horses	Pleasure Carriages
BOWLING, Edmund									
BROWN, John									
BOWLING, Edm. Sr.	100	L.C.	deeded						
BRYAN, John Jr.					1				
BRYAN, William					1				
CONWAY, Wm. Maj.	365	C.R.					8		1-2W
COATNEY, George	406	B.M.					2		
COATNEY, James	250	B.M.			1				
COATNEY, Fielding									
CATCHING, John	459	L.C.			1				
CROSBY, George	700	L.C.	deeded						
CROSBY, Wm. Decd.	166								
DUNIGAN, Nicholas									
DAVIS, Jos. Esqr.	310	L.C.					3		
DAVIS, Nathan	200	L.C.			1				
DYER, Abraham Dcd.	165								
DYER, Jacob	200	W.L.			1				
DAVIS, Leeland	100				1				
DYER, John					1				
FIELDING, Jesse	83	B.M.							
FAIN, John	2				1				
GORDON, Robert C.	200	L.C.	deed						
GAMMONS, John K.									
GLASCOCK, George					1				
GASS, Alexander									
HURLEY, Zachariah	490				1				
HURLEY, Joseph	313								
HAWN, Christr. Sr.	588½	L.C.							
HAWN, John	42	L.C.							
HALE, Joseph	216	L.C.			1		2		
HALE, Pat. Decd.	346	C.R.			1		3		
HAWN, Christr. Jr.	36				1				
HAWN, Daniel					1				
HALE, Thomas S.	267				1		3		
HOLLOWY, Henry					1				
KIRK, Henry					1				
KESTERSON, Sn.									
KESTERSON, Chas.					1				
KESTERSON, Wm.	100								
KESTERSON, Thos.	132	L.C.			1				
KESTERSON, John					1				
KELLER, Jacob					1				
LANDRUM, Jas. Rev.		L.C.							
LUSTER, William									
LUSTER, Joseph									
LUSTER, Mary									
LANHAM, Cluffy					1				

Persons Names	Quantity of Land in Each Tract	Situation or Place Where Each Tract Lies	Material Circumstances of the Title	Common School Lands	No. of White Polls	No. of Town Lots	No. of Slaves	No. of Stud Horses	Pleasure Carriages
MATTHEWS, James	173	B.M.							
MATTHEWS, William	280	B.M.	deeded						
MURRAY, George	197	B.C.			1		3		
MYERS, Elizabeth									
MILLER, Samuel	150	L.C.	deeded		1				
McINTOSH, Abel	96						3		
MYERS, Wilson					1				
MATTHEWS, Nancy	30								
McMILLIAN, Jere.					1				
MATTHEWS, Jas. Jr.									
MASSY, Josiah					1				
McMILLIAN, John					1				
NEILSON, Wm. D.									
NEILSON, Patrick									
NEILSON, Horatio									
NEILSON, Joseph H.									
NEILSON, George									
NEWEL, John	20				1				
NEWEL, Joseph	130				1				
NEWEL, David					1				
NEWEL, William					1				
PETTIT, Nehemiah Decd.	130	L.C.							
PETTIT, William									
PETTIT, Joel					1				
PETTIT, Susanna	60	L.C.	deeded						
REED, Matthias									
REED, Solomon	400		deeded		1				
RIPPETOE, Thos. B.									
SENTERY, William	290								
SMITH, Robert					1				
SCOTT, Elijah									
STROUD, Thomas	96		deeded		1				
SENTER, James					1				
TRAIL, Archibald									
TRAIL, James					1				
VOYLES, Henry									
WHITE, Joseph	210							1	1 $2
WISECARVER, John	81	L.C.	deeded						
WATKINS, by agent Wm. CORRAY									
WISE, Benjamin									
WILKERSON, Richard	100				1				
WARD, Enoch	100				1				

By Jas. DAVIS, J. P.

Copies of the foregoing tax lists delivered No. 1 to John Allison Esqr. – 26th Nov. 1830, and No. 2 to No. 18 – both inclusive – to R. M. Woods Shff. – 30th Nov. 1830.